To
H.A.P.

THE VISIONARY LANDSCAPE

A STUDY IN MEDIEVAL ALLEGORY

Paul Piehler

EDWARD ARNOLD

First published 1971 by
Edward Arnold (Publishers) Ltd
41 Maddox Street, London W 1

ISBN: 0 7131 5579 5

Printed in Great Britain
by W & J Mackay & Co Ltd, Chatham

Contents

I   INTRODUCTION

Allegory and Myth   1
Definitions of Terms   8
Nine Propositions   19

2   THE SEMINAL IMAGES

Invocations   21
Techniques of Control   27

3   BOETHIUS

Philosophical Dialogue   31
Lady Philosophy   34
Cosmic Alienation   41
Allegory and Symbolism   42

4   ALAN'S VISION OF NATURE

The Coming of Lady Nature   47
Cosmos and Morality   52
The Therapeutic Dialogue   62
Is Sex Necessary?   67

5   THE LANDSCAPES OF VISION

The Sacred Places   70
The Psychology of Landscape: Wilderness and City   72
The Sources of Allegorical Landscape   78

6   LANDSCAPE AND DIALOGUE

The *Architrenius*   85
Parodies of Love   94
Guillaume de Lorris: The Secret Garden   98
Jean's *Roman*: The Garden Invaded   105

7   DANTE

The *Selva Selvaggia*   111
The Vergilian Categories   117
The Redemption of Images   122
Dante's Dialogues   134
The Figure of Beatrice   138

8   PEARL

The *Erber Grene*   144
The Artifice of Eternity   146
The Pearl Maiden   154

CONCLUSION   163

INDEX   165

Acknowledgments

My first inspiration towards the study of visionary allegory arose from my association with C. S. Lewis and J. A. W. Bennett at Magdalen College, Oxford. I have also greatly benefited from the advice and counsel of Professors W. H. Jackson, William Nelson, A. Kent Hieatt, and Howard Schless, in developing these ideas while undergoing graduate studies at Columbia University. I should particularly like to stress the value to me of the encouragement and good counsel of Professors Charles Muscatine and Philip Damon of the University of California at Berkeley in the final stages of rendering down some of my experiences with medieval allegory into the form of a publishable manuscript. The collaboration and assistance of Professor Winthrop Wetherbee, particularly with reference to the profounder aspects of twelfth-century Latin vision poetry, has been essential to my understanding of this period. In revising and reshaping the manuscript the help of many friends should be acknowledged, especially that of George Bland, Theodore Bogdanos, Ronald Brady, Anne Henderson, Eric Kline, Elizabeth Petroff, and Myrtle Raj.

Grateful acknowledgement for permission to quote is made to the following: Noonday Press for a passage from W. H. Auden's preface to *The Visionary Novels of George Macdonald*; Prentice Hall for a passage from Wayne Shumaker, *Literature and the Irrational*; the Clarendon Press for quotations from Cyril Bailey, "Religion and Philosophy", in *The Legacy of Rome*, from R. J. Werblowsky, *Joseph Karo, Lawyer and Mystic*, and from *Pearl*, edited by E. V. Gordon; Princeton University Press for passages from E. R. Curtius, *European Literature and the Latin Middle Ages*, from *The Collected Works of C. G. Jung* volumes 5 and 9, from C. G. Jung and C. Kerenyi, *Essays on a Science of Mythology*, and from Northrop Frye, "Allegory" in *Encyclopedia of Poetry and Poetics*; Routledge & Kegan Paul for passages from C. G. Jung, *Modern Man in Search of a Soul* and *Contributions to Analytical Psychology*; The University of Chicago Press for a quotation from Arnold van Gennep, *The Rites of Passage*, translated by Monika

Vizedom; Yale University Press for material from Ernst Cassirer, *An Essay on Man.*

I am particularly grateful to my father, H. A. Piehler, for his Daedalian skill in handling the labyrinthine problems of the index.

Introduction

ALLEGORY AND MYTH

T HIS book is concerned with the manifestations of a certain type of psychic experience in medieval literature. The experience itself is a very widespread one, by no means confined to the Middle Ages, though it attained at that time its most sophisticated literary expression. Before defining this experience, let us look at two widely separated instances of its occurrence. The first of these occurred to a certain Sumerian priest-king, Gudea of Lagash, at the beginning of the second millennium B.C. Disturbed by the failure of the Tigris to rise and irrigate the fields at the proper time, Gudea took the normal course of a Sumerian ruler in such a crisis and went to sleep in the temple of the responsible deity. His "incubation" was rewarded by an impressive but enigmatic dream, which (since he was evidently unable or unqualified to interpret it for himself) he related to a minor goddess, Nanshe, who specialized in dream interpretations. Here is his account:

> To Nanshe he went, saluted her:
> "Nanshe, queen, priestess,
> queen who 'decides the fates' like the god Enlil,
> my Nanshe, you who, since your word is irrefutable,
> precedent-making,
> are the *ensi*-priestess of the gods,
> are the queen of all countries, mother, discuss with
>   me the dream:
> In the dream, the first man—like the heaven was his
>   surpassing size,
> like the earth was his surpassing size,
> according to his horn-crowned head he was a god,
> according to his wings he was Imdugud the
>   bird of the Weather-god,
> according to his lower parts he was the Storm-flood,

lions were lying to his right and left—
commanded me to build his house;
but I do not know what he had in mind.
Daylight rose for me on the horizon.
The first woman—whoever she may have been—
coming out ahead did . . .
a stylus she held in her hand,
a tablet of heavenly stars she put on her knees,
consulting it.
The second man was a warrior,
a tablet of lapis lazuli he held in his hand,
set down thereon the plan of the temple.
Before me stood a pure carrying pad,
a pure brick-mould was lined up,
a brick, determined as to its nature, was placed in
    the mould for me,
in a conduit standing before me
was a slosher, a bird-man, keeping clear
    water flowing,
a male donkey at the right of my lord
kept pawing the ground for me."[1]

Nanshe has no difficulties in making a consistent interpretation. Each detail of the dream symbolizes the role of some minor god who would play his part in building the new temple commanded by the major god, Ningirsu. The daylight was Gudea's personal god (or, as we might say, vital energy, conceived of as a force outside volitional control). The woman with the tablet was the goddess of wisdom and astrology who would determine the correct time for beginning the work, and so on all the way to the donkey, who represents, rather unflatteringly one might think, Gudea himself in his capacity as eager and obedient servant of the god. Gudea is satisfied with the interpretation but is still unclear in his mind about certain details; however, after a further incubation and interpretation he is able to go ahead and have the temple built successfully.

The second experience is also a dream, recorded nearly four thousand years later by a professional man who had been worried

---

[1] Translation based on version by Th. Jacobsen, in A. Leo Oppenheim, "The Interpretation of Dreams in the Ancient Near East", *Transactions of the American Philosophical Society* 46 (1956), pp. 245–6. For detailed discussion of "incubation" see the above work, especially pp. 188–91.

about his sanity and was at the time undergoing psychoanalytic treatment.

"I am entering a solemn house. It is called 'the house of inner composure or self-collection'. In the background are many burning candles arranged so as to form four pyramid-like points. An old man stands at the door of the house. People enter, they do not talk and often stand still in order to concentrate. The old man at the door tells me about the visitors to the house and says: 'When they leave they are pure.' I enter the house now, and I am able to concentrate completely. A voice says: 'What thou art doing is dangerous. Religion is not a tax which thou payest in order to get rid of the woman's image, for this image is indispensable. Woe to those who use religion as a substitute for the other side of the soul's life. They are in error and they shall be cursed. Religion is no substitute, but it is the ultimate accomplishment added to every other activity of the soul. Out of the fulness of life thou shalt give birth to thy religion, only then shalt thou be blessed.' Together with the last sentence a faint music becomes audible, simple tunes played by an organ, reminding me somewhat of Wagner's 'fire magic' [*Feuerzauber*]. As I leave the house I have the vision of a flaming mountain and I feel that a fire that cannot be quenched must be a sacred fire."

The analyst commented on the dreamer's attitude towards his experience:

The patient is deeply impressed by the dream. It is a solemn and far-reaching experience to him, one of several which produced a complete change in his attitude to life and humanity.

The analyst, like Nanshe, also made an elaborate and interesting interpretation of each of the individual images of the dream (the old man, the candles, the flaming mountain, etc.), as well as of its general significance to the life and problems of the dreamer.[2]

The two experiences, each apparently typical of its period, have a number of significant similarities. Each dreamer was faced by an alarming problem that set up considerable emotional tension and was felt to be beyond his volitional/conscious control. In each case the initial answer to the problem was provided by an enigmatic vision of a psychic "authority" in a place with sacred associations. In each case, though he was able to make some preliminary assessment of the significance of his experience, the dreamer had to

[2] C. G. Jung, *Psychology and Religion* (Yale, 1938), pp. 42*ff*.

obtain further elucidation from an appropriate interpreter. Thus in each case an event which is too complex for the dreamer to deal with is presented to him in two different ways: as a vision embodying appropriate symbolic images conventional to the society in question, and as a rational analysis of this symbolic imagery.

There are also significant divergences between the visions. While in both cases the dreamer made a response to the vision typical for his time and place, the Sumerian *ensi* (and his later Akkadian and Assyrian counterparts) tended to attach most significance to dreams prompted by crises that we should associate, in principle at least, with happenings in "the external world": an invasion, civil war, plague, unfortunate conjunction of planets, etc.[3] The dream, in modern theories, is assumed to be an event purely on the psychic plane. The external troubles of modern society are no longer felt as sufficiently complex and overwhelming to require resort to visions; instead they are dealt with by purely external authorities on rational principles. Priest and prophet have given way to bureaucrat and politician.

These two visions define the characteristics of the kind of medieval allegory we are concerned with here—allegory as a manifestation of this particular type of mental experience, which we may term visionary allegory. Most important medieval allegories fall into this category: typically the dreamer is profoundly disturbed by some spiritual crisis;[4] he has a vision of mysterious import which is interpreted by persons in spiritual authority, and the effect of the vision and its interpretation is to resolve the crisis, often by raising him to a higher spiritual state. As we might expect, these medieval visions are intermediate in character between the two visions we have been discussing. The dreamer does not have the status in his society of a Sumerian *ensi*, an Egyptian pharaoh, or a tribal shaman. On the other hand he is by no means a mere private individual, like the modern dreamer of significant dreams. As a poet he still has something of the role of the priest, prophet or *vates*, as we can see very clearly in Dante's attitude to the figure of Vergil in the *Divine Comedy*. While medieval visionary allegories are chiefly concerned with crises of the spirit rather than with external problems of society, yet these crises pertain to the spiritual

[3] See Oppenheim, especially pp. 184–5.
[4] *Cf.* Professor Angus Fletcher on anxiety, in *Allegory, The Theory of a Symbolic Mode* (Cornell, 1964), p. 37.

4

problems of society as much as to those of specific individuals. Moreover, the allegories differ sharply from modern accounts of such visions in that they are offered to their readers for spiritual participation, so that in undergoing the imaginative experience of the vision they may avail themselves of the same process of healing and transcendence.

While many pre-medieval visions included advice or commands from a venerable person or a god, the interpretation of the vision was normally entrusted to professional dream interpreters. In the vision of Gudea it appears likely that the interpretations of Nanshe were given by a priestess of the goddess, rather than being revealed in a dream or trance. We are familiar with the role of dream interpreter to the king played by the Biblical figures of Joseph and Daniel. But in medieval allegory, the interpretation of the vision is normally entrusted to the figure of authority within the vision itself. Such interpretation, drawing on the tradition of the philosophical dialogue, often becomes sufficiently elaborate and complex as to constitute the most important element of the visionary experience.[5]

The approach of the present work to the allegorical visions of the Middle Ages is twofold. So far as literary history is concerned, it attempts an elucidation of medieval allegory in terms of its most important antecedents: the ancient myths out of which developed its central imagery, and the classical dialogue, which contributed the basis of its intellectual structure. Concurrently, it seeks to interpret visionary allegory as a profound and far-reaching exploration of the human psyche, sustained and developed for over a thousand years. Such interpretation is not always easy to harmonize with the work of the literary historian; but an appreciation of the aesthetic value of a mode of artistic expression needs to be based not only on historical scholarship but also on earnest consideration of the main intentions of the artist, however remote from scholarly ways of thought his intentions may be.

[5] C. G. Jung describes the "visionary mode" of literature as "a strange something that derives its existence from the hinterland of man's mind—that suggests the abyss of time separating us from pre-human ages, or evokes a super-human world of contrasting light and darkness. It is a primordial experience which surpasses man's understanding, and to which he is therefore in danger of succumbing." (*Modern Man in Search of a Soul*, New York, 1933, pp. 156–7.) It is typically the function of the element of dialogue in medieval allegory to enable the poet and his readers to face and control the dæmonic force represented in the pure "visionary" or mythic experience.

What then has medieval allegory to tell us about the human psyche? In 1938 Carl Jung wrote of the patient, one of whose dreams we have just been discussing:

> The modern mind has forgotten those old truths that speak of the death of the old man and of the making of a new one, of spiritual rebirth and similar old-fashioned "mystical absurdities". My patient, being a scientist of today, was more than once seized by panic when he realized how much he was gripped by such thoughts. He was afraid of becoming insane, whereas the man of two thousand years ago would have welcomed such dreams and rejoiced in the hope of a magical rebirth and renewal of life. But our modern attitude looks back proudly upon the mists of superstition and of medieval or primitive credulity and entirely forgets that it carries the whole living past in the lower stories of the skyscraper of rational consciousness. Without the lower stories our mind is suspended in mid-air. No wonder that it gets nervous. The true history of the mind is not preserved in learned volumes but in the living mental organism of everyone.[6]

Even before Jung had written these words, however, much had already been done to restore connections with the forgotten "lower stories", as seen, for example, in the mythological dimensions of the work of two of the best known poets of his day, T. S. Eliot and Yeats. In the last forty years, not only have the psychoanalysts been accepted into the framework of society as a kind of auxiliary priesthood, but the links between psychology and literature have been strengthened by psychological scrutiny of myth and literature by such Jungians as Maud Bodkin and Erich Neumann, and the literary man's use of the psychologist's findings on myth by such writers as Northrop Frye and W. H. Auden.

Nonetheless the relation of medieval allegory to myth has been left largely unexplored.[7] While it has been generally recognized that medieval exegetical allegory was extensively applied to pagan myth as well as to Biblical texts, this type of allegorizing has never been taken seriously as comment on myth as such; generally speaking, it has been considered to have no more than a certain local significance as throwing light on the vagaries of the "medieval mind". Its importance certainly is secondary, but secondary to the

[6] C. G. Jung, *Psychology and Religion*, p. 41.
[7] *Cf.*, however, J. A. Stewart, *The Myths of Plato* (London, 1960), p. 213.

really significant allegorizing of ancient myth, carried out as a new and higher type of mythopœia by the greatest poets of the Middle Ages. We have thus failed to understand the central significance of medieval allegory and to exploit its proper potentiality as the highroad by which the heritage of ancient myth has been made available to the modern world. To understand myth, and the role and function of the persons and places of the mythical world within one's own personality, it is insufficient merely to be acquainted with classical or pre-classical myth-making. Since every age has had new and creative interpretations to make of the ancient motifs, we need to understand the complete history of myth to the present day.

But it is particularly perilous to neglect the medieval handling of myth. For modern man is not so much concerned with the mythical for its own sake, as with the function of the mythical and intuitional elements in the human consciousness as they relate to and interact with the rational elements of his psychic life. The particular contribution of the Middle Ages was to achieve a type of mythopœia in which neither the pre-rational intuitive elements nor the reason had excessive domination. Medieval allegory at its best achieved a balance of rational and intuitive elements, an acceptance of all levels on which the mind functions, which is the goal of those who seek psychic integration today.

The scope of this work does not include all medieval allegory, nor indeed, all those works which may fairly be termed visionary dialogues. I do not treat here a greater number of allegories than sufficient to illustrate the more important characteristics and developments of the medieval visionary dialogue, though I step outside this genre to illustrate, from the *psychomachia* for example, features which can be better explained in light of another tradition.

Any attempt to present theories about complex, multidimensional allegories in a single-dimensioned exposition must result in a work of quite imperfect arrangement. In an attempt to simplify the reader's task of following my argument, I treat each allegory under the following categories: the preliminary anguish; the subsequent prayers and invocations by which the hero of the allegory obtains access to the visionary world; the *loci*, the landscapes and habitations, of this world; the character of the chief person or persons he meets there; the dialogue which ensues between the hero and these persons. The order of topics outlined here is an ideal one; visionary allegory is sufficiently variable in construction to make it necessary to depart from this order on occasion. Sometimes, for example, where an allegory contains a number of separate scenes or events it is more convenient to treat these as separate allegories.

DEFINITION OF TERMS

Unfortunately no systematic vocabulary has yet been developed for the discussion and analysis of medieval allegory. The literary historian must therefore either continually attempt to stretch the vocabulary of modern literary discussion to fit the phenomena of medieval thought, or attempt to develop a special vocabulary himself, thereby running the risk of creating an unnecessary and perhaps incomprehensible jargon. In the present work, the second choice seems the lesser of the two evils, and I therefore offer notice here of the specialized terms I am obliged to use. In each case I shall indicate briefly what I understand to be the regular modern usage of the term in question, and attempt a redefinition of that usage required by this interpretation of medieval allegory.

Symbolism and the pre-rational. The concept of symbolism is employed here in two differing but related senses. In the literary analysis of allegory, the symbolic aspects are seen as those which represent intuitive elements as they exist in the human mind prior to being acted on—identified and controlled—by the rational functions. These more primitive elements typically carry a strong imaginative and emotional impact which cannot be explicated in rational terms without a major loss in the significance of what is symbolized.

When allegory is considered from the historical point of view, however, the symbolic aspects are best understood in terms of their development from the mythological imagery of western culture, since such imagery embodies the pre-rational elements of our thought as they existed prior to their subjection to extensive rational analysis by allegorists, creative and exegetical. The historical process thus demonstrates on the broad canvas of history the psychological processes underlying literary symbolism. In this

8

aspect, the present work reflects a judgment about the pre-rational elements in literature first put forward by Wayne Shumaker in *Literature and the Irrational* (Englewood Cliffs, N.J., 1960).

Our subject has been irrationality in art, and particularly in literature; and in the greater number of pages evidence has been offered for a belief that the source of the irrationality is a tendency to recapture the perceptual and reflective habits of primitive men and of children. From the beginning, however, it has been implicit that nonrational psychic states are impregnated with feeling—that, in fact, they depend heavily upon it, that their dynamic structure is largely determined by it. When the mind does not stand coolly off from experience to conceptualize it, but instead flows into it undivided and whole, as among children and savages, the resulting image of the world derives in considerable part from the patterns of the affections themselves. (p. 263)

The historical and literary dimensions of symbolism are inseparable in medieval allegory; it is only due to later developments that literary symbolism took on a separate existence. Ultimately, therefore, we may reduce the irrational element in symbolism to the pre-rational character of the primitive mind—an irrationality neither capricious, nor arbitrarily mysterious.

Since the manifestations of the irrational in medieval allegory are almost exclusively primitive and mythopœic in character we term them pre-rational, leaving the term *irrational* for the deliberately non-rational expressions of later poets and artists. We shall also distinguish an important subdivision of the pre-rational as the anti-rational, since we shall find ourselves involved with some highly significant mythical and allegorical literature which represents and enacts the irruptive assaults of aggressively anti-rational psychic forces on the rational stability of the human soul. As such representations demonstrate very clearly the allegorist's role as interpreter and controller of pre-rational elements in the human psyche, we shall examine these *psychomachia* in the next chapter. It should also be noted that while the terms *anti-rational* and *irrational* are absolute in that they represent a definite tendency to turn away, in a controlled or uncontrolled fashion, from reason, the term *pre-rational* is merely relative, since the process of depicting a psychic event in terms of persons or events from the external world is controlled by shaping processes whose method and function is analogous to later and more sophisticated rational processes.

9

Allegory as a genre. In a recent discussion of allegory, Northrop Frye points out that "works usually called allegories are genres of fiction", epic, romance, drama, etc., and (one might add) the genre of the dialogue.[8] There is considerable truth in this: strictly speaking, allegory is not so much a genre itself as something that happens to other forms of literature. However, I find it difficult to agree with Frye's conclusion that allegory is therefore a "structural principle in fiction". It would be difficult to demonstrate, for example, that the *Faerie Queene* differs in respect of structural principles from the Italian romances to which it owes much of its form. In fact, it is just the basing of an allegory quite rigidly on the Italianate epic structures that constitutes much of what is remarkable and important in the form of the *Faerie Queene*. What defines visionary allegory up to the Renaissance is its utilization of the images of the external world and the structural principles of some genre such as the classical dialogue, to shape a visionary world in which spiritual powers can be encountered and portrayed directly. Where in primitive myth there is no distinction between external form and internal spiritual significance, in allegory we find a deliberate attempt, dependent on both the intuitive and the rational operations of the mind, to reinvest the external world with this lost internal dimension, in order to gain access to and participate in the acquisition of important spiritual truths.

Once this has been granted one may admit that a general class, of dubious authenticity, has been made out of all the literary works transformed in this manner, which has been termed allegory. This class might better have been termed vision poetry; indeed the reason for its being called allegory is an interesting history itself, one which will be touched on in the next section. However, it would seem better to attempt to recover something of the true significance of the word allegory, rather than make a confusing fresh start with a new term.

Allegory proper. Having with some hesitation accepted allegory as the name of a genre of literature, we must turn from its substantive to its adjectival aspect, to allegory as a type of writing. Allegory proper pleases by the appropriateness, ingenuity and wit displayed in the translation of the basic material into allegorical

[8] Article "Allegory" in *Encyclopaedia of Poetry and Poetics* (Princeton, 1965), p. 12.

form. Allegory in this sense is to be distinguished from symbolism, whose ancient and profound images are less readily interpretable in rational terms. The double use of the term allegory is by no means convenient; the one use encompasses everything to be found in a work of literature with an allegorical dimension, the other only the purest, at times over-refined, allegorical writing. But at this point of time one can only attempt to clarify the distinction. The second meaning arose historically from the fact that in the eighteenth century allegory became separated from its function of representing the spiritual world in terms of external phenomena, and concentrated merely on the representation of abstract ideas. This led to Coleridge's famous and influential definition (in the *Statesman's Manual*) of allegory as the translation of a non-poetic structure, usually of abstract ideas, into poetic imagery.[9] This quite damning definition was certainly justified as a description of contemporary allegory but has distorted our understanding of pre-eighteenth-century allegory up to the present time.

However, there is one element in the complex literary phenomenon of medieval allegory which in some sense answers to Coleridge's definition; indeed were there not it would have been impossible for the misunderstandings to have arisen. This, since it constitutes the most distinctively and exclusively allegorical element, we may call allegory proper. It arises basically from the interplay of the rational mind and the mythical, symbolic and intuitional elements, and manifests itself as a type of symbolism in which the symbolic element is translatable with relative directness into rational terms. In medieval allegory, however, as opposed to that of the eighteenth century, this rational element is only one dimension of a very complex symbolic pattern, and is only distinguishable from it in what one might term a Coleridgean analysis.

The image. A recent writer discussing the use of the image in literature makes three classifications: the simple depiction of sense impression in words, the image regarded as a figure of speech, and

[9] (Coleridge, *Complete Works*, edited by W. T. Shedd, New York, 1884, pp. 437–8). The question of the relationship of medieval allegory to symbolism is not accounted for even in C. S. Lewis's *Allegory of Love* (Oxford, 1936, pp. 44ff.), which still suffers from the misleading effects of Coleridge's remarks. An attempt at a more plausible formulation of the relationship will be found in chapter 3.

images and image patterns regarded as embodiments of "symbolic vision" or of "non-discursive truth". The third of these classifications is especially concerned with images as "tone setters, structural devices, and symbols", and with their relationship to myths and rituals.[10] The image, as the term will be employed in this work, should normally be understood in accordance with the third of these categories.

But a nearer definition of the image as used in medieval allegory can be found in the Latin usage of *imago* or the Greek *eidolon*, words which embrace simultaneously such meanings as mental image, spirit or apparition, appearance of respected deceased ancestor, and intellectual idea or concept.[11] A composite definition might read: a description of a traditional figure or its locale, carrying specific symbolical and intellectual overtones of meaning.

The persons of the visionary dialogue: the potentiae. We need a specific name for the *imagines* or *eidola* described above when they appear specifically as active influential powers, in the form of a divinity, personification, or figure of authority. Insofar as they hold a dialogue with the poet, they may be termed Mistresses (or Masters) of Discourse. But though this role is so frequent as to be almost definitive, it constitutes their major function rather than their essential nature. Socrates is the greatest of all Masters of Discourse, but he is certainly not an *imago* in the sense that the Scipio Africanus of the *Somnium Scipionis* can be said to be an *imago*, for he does not appear on a plane of purely mental or psychic reality, in dream or vision. Statius' *Clementia* in the *Thebaid* (book XII) or Chaucer's Venus in the *Parlement of Foules* are obviously *imagines*, though they never actually hold discourse. We need a phrase that will cover such diverse manifestations of the *imago* figure as Athene, *Natura*, *Philosophia*, Beatrice, and the visionary St. Augustine of Plutarch's *Secretum*. Modern criticism seems to have little to say about such figures; the nearest we can get to it is Jung's archetype of the Wise Old Man—sexually a rare mutànt among the generally

---

[10] Norman Friedman in *Encyclopaedia of Poetry and Poetics*, pp. 363–4, 368; also René Wellek and Austin Warren, *Theory of Literature* (New York, 1956), pp. 176–7.

[11] *Cf.* Cicero's account of the Epicurean concept in *De Finibus* I. VI. 21: ". . . imagines, quae *eidola* nominant, quorum incursione non solum videamus, sed etiam cogitemus. . . ." The image and the conception are fused into a single concept.

feminine *imagines* of the medieval psyche. If the medievals had had
to find a name for such a figure, they might well have termed it
potentia animae, which preserves a necessary ambiguity as to the
origin of the *potentia*—as to whether the power controls the mind
from within or without.[12]

Settings of the allegories: the loci. The *potentia animae* is represented
as existing not in the void one might at first consider appropriate
for an interior *imago*, but almost invariably in a setting which, like
the *potentiae* themselves, is composed of images taken from the
external world and transfigured by spiritual vision. The external
images selected for this function are manifold—forests, cities,
gardens, temples, prisons. The setting inevitably constitutes an
essential dimension of the meaning of the figure, whether by way of
reinforcement, or more rarely, contrast. Once more it seems difficult to find anything useful in modern scholarship to describe these
varied manifestations with any adequacy. The nearest useful term
is Mircea Eliade's "Sacred Place", as analysed in more primitive
cultures, but such a term would be misleading as applied to the
imagines of medieval culture, for many of the places, like many
of the *potentiae*, are no longer sacred in medieval times but quite
provocatively profane.[13] I therefore propose to use the more general
and uncoloured term *locus*, or more fully, *locus animae*, in the belief
that since one of the pleasant manifestations of this *imago* is termed
locus amoenus in this period, a special use of *locus* to indicate the
whole genus of such places is not excessively unmedieval in spirit.

[12] The term *potentia* is employed by Bernandus Silvestris to describe the
pagan gods, in their role as psychological forces: " 'Quantum ad interiorem
intellectum *deas* vocat animi potentias, *errantes* quia in primis aetatibus
erraverint, *agitata* commotionibus carnis. *Phebo* hactenus preces et modo
vota sapientiae. . . .' (In respect of the inner mind, he [Vergil] calls the
'powers' of the soul *goddesses—wandering* because in the primal ages they
wandered around, disturbed by the agitations of the flesh. By 'to Phoebus'
here we understand simply prayers and vows to Wisdom.)" *Commentum*
(on *Aeneid* VI.68) edited by Riedel (Gryphiswaldae, 1924), pp. 46–7. The
term *potestas* is employed in a similar manner, perhaps after N. T. usage,
as in *I Peter* III.22 etc. In the *Visio Sancti Pauli* (edited by Theodore
Silverstein, London, 1935, pp. 131–3) *potestas* is the term denoting
spiritual powers that challenge the soul after death, as to his right to enter
heaven. Chalcidius refers to *Natura, Fortuna,* and *Casus* as *potestates* and
daemones, spiritual beings, in his *Commentarius* on the *Timaeus*, edited by
J. H. Waszink (London, 1962), p. 188.

[13] See Mircea Eliade, *Patterns in Comparative Religion* (New York,
1963), chapter x.

Imago and archetype. It might well be questioned whether all this laborious definition is necessary when Jung and the Jungian critics have already popularized the term "archetype" for such widely occurring mental images. However, a little scrutiny will show that the best use of this concept in discussing medieval allegory is likely to be adjectival rather than substantive.

A modern writer defines the archetype as "containing essential characteristics which are primitive, general, and universal, rather than sophisticated, unique, and particular", its universality comprehending not only literary works, but folk tales, myths, dreams and rituals.[14] On the other hand, while the allegorical *imago* is in one aspect primitive and universal, in its specific allegorical treatment it is often highly sophisticated, unique, and particular.

I shall therefore employ the adjective "archetypal" only in the analysis of the primitive or mythical aspects of the *imago*, much of its importance lying in the quality of its relationship to the more sophisticated elements. It will not be employed as a mere synonym for "primitive" or "mythical". The most precise and meaningful use of the term is, I feel, to designate the residue of elements in a figure, event or situation, which cannot be accounted for in any other terms than the archetypal—a universally occurring pattern of ritualized transmutation of reality which defies further explication. It should not be used merely to indicate elements that are explicable in the light of the development of myth into allegory where direct literary borrowing seems evident. By employing the word "archetypal", the literary historian confesses in fact that he has little more of practical value to say in description of the *imago*, since, for him as for the practising psychoanalyst, the archetype becomes significant only in relation to the particular subject he is examining. Thus any useful explanation of the archetype must necessarily move away from the general to the particular circumstances of its manifestation.

This use of the word therefore does not imply acceptance of any general thesis of the origin or nature of archetypes. It is not necessary

[14] Article "Archetype" in *Encyclopaedia of Poetry and Poetics*, p. 48. My use of *imago* is not too distant from Jung's early use of this term. *Cf. Symbols of Transformation* (New York, 1956), p. 44: "Here I purposely give preference to the term 'imago' rather than to 'complex', in order to make clear, by this choice of a technical term, that the psychological factor which I sum up under 'imago' has a living independence in the psychic hierarchy, i.e., possesses that *autonomy* which wide experience has shown to be the essential feature of feeling-toned complexes."

for the literary historian to pass judgment on the validity of the Jungian thesis of their origin as "an uprush from the collective unconscious", since such phrasing, however valuable in psychological theory, can hardly by its nature be helpful in explicating particular literary situations. An alternate Jungian theory, however, describes archetypes as "the formulated resultants of countless typical experiences of our ancestors. They are, as it were, the psychic residua of numberless experiences of the same type."[15] This explanation is clearly inapplicable to the manifestation of goddesses in transcendent landscapes which constitutes the central psychic experience in medieval allegory. Such experiences can never, by definition, have occurred to anyone in normal, waking experience, let alone have occurred numberless times. The element of spiritual transformation, which alone permits us to identify an experience as archetypal, is left out of account in such an explanation.

Seminal image. In pagan religious rites, the preliminary to the manifestation of the deity was an elaborate process of nomination and evocation, translating him from a mere awareness of a desire for his presence to the full participation in the spiritual state he expresses and manifests. Surprisingly, the structure of such pagan ritual remains, with only slight modification, in the structure of allegory right up to the sixteenth century. Typically, a medieval allegory enacts the transformation of some bare personification or other static and unstructured image into a full visionary *potentia* in its appropriate *locus*. This conversion, as fits with the origins of allegory in the visions of troubled shamans, is almost invariably carried out under conditions of considerable mental anguish on the part of the poet, an anguish which can only be relieved by the manifestation of the beneficent *potentia animae*. Since previous recognition and analysis of this allegorical phenomenon seems lacking, I have arbitrarily named the *imago* in its preliminary or invocatory state, a "seminal image".

Allegorical analysis. The seminal image or images of an allegory (or other major topics not necessarily appearing in imagery) are subjected to what one may term allegorical analysis. This differs from the analytic methods to which we are accustomed today in

---

[15] "On the Relation of Analytical Psychology to Poetic Art" in *Contributions to Analytical Psychology* (London, 1928), p. 246.

that there occurs not only rational exegesis of the subject in question (normally in the form of a dialogue), but also a creative development and expansion of the basic image into its potential imagistic components.[16] In the hands of a great poet this process is capable of extraordinarily powerful and subtle effects; it reaches its culmination in the *Commedia* where the development of imagery recapitulates the total historical development of imagery within man's psyche, at least so far as we can trace such development at the present time.

Tradition. The majority of the allegorists whose visions are described below seem to have had a strong feeling for the thought and imagery of their predecessors, as well as a strong desire to do justice to and advance their predecessors' work, by treating it in a somewhat different light, or taking into account further relevant factors, and by incorporating their contributions into a larger whole.

This description might well sound more appropriate to a group of scientific investigators than to creators of imaginative literature. The parallel is a revealing one. The medieval allegorist undoubtedly ascribed not the same type of validity but certainly the same intensity of validity to his experiences of and thought about his chosen field of investigation as the modern scientist. It was an age philosophically (and psychologically) "realistic" in ascribing relatively greater reality to "universals" or general concepts than we do today, and psychologically more "realistic" in its ability to enter into direct communication with such universals in the guise of the *potentia* of allegorical poetry. Nor were the medievals any less adept at giving equivalent validity to the mythical beings, the gentile gods who were the psychological ancestors as well as contemporaries of the allegorical entities who embodied the universals. In spite of their religious presuppositions, the medievals were far too deeply concerned with the world of the psyche to throw out the magnificent body of psychological theory embodied in the myths of the classical pantheon.

Psychological postulates. This work does not attempt to make any analysis as such of the human psyche of the medieval, or any other, period. But some theory of the psyche has to be presupposed for

[16] Allegory as a mode of analysis is not an aspect of its functions that seems to have been much commented on by critics. But *cf.* J. A. Stewart, *The Myths of Plato*, p. 378.

any serious study of literature, and it is easier to avoid misunderstandings if the theory is so far as possible made explicit.

The mind can function as an organ for the perception of autonomous psychic powers, felt as external to the perceiver but making their appearances (in the Middle Ages at least) chiefly in the perceiver's internal world—the world of vision and dream.[17] They manifest themselves in the form of images drawn from the external world but enhanced and transfigured by an infusion of spiritual meaning. This transfiguration may be regarded, in the light of certain contemporary theories of the development of consciousness, as a recapturing of an original spiritual vision of man, in which the phenomena and values of the internal and external world were identified in a state of fusion and wholeness.[18] Some though not all

[17] The avowedly sceptical and rationalistic atomic theory of Democritus had evidently to take account of the persistent visions of the gods in dreams in his period, explaining them as atomized *eidola* emanating from persons and objects and making their way into the mind of a dreamer through a physical penetration of the pores of the body. E. R. Dodds (*The Greeks and the Irrational*, Berkeley, 1963, pp. 117–18) regards Democritus's theory as "an attempt to provide a mechanistic basis for the objective dream", that is, the ancient belief that the dream is an objective entity wandering amongst men, a belief that was rejected by Aristotle (*On Prophesying by Dreams* 464A, 5) and Cicero (*Acad. Quaest.* 2. XL.125), but still finds scientific acceptance in Lucretius (*De Nat. Rerum* V.1161ff.), and poetic acceptance (via Ovid) as late as Chaucer's *Book of the Duchess* (135–211). For medieval dreams, see Philip W. Damon, *Twelfth Century Latin Vision Poetry* (dissertation, University of California, 1952), chapter 1, especially p. 8. "He [Cyprian] often refers to his practice of making these visions a rule of life; the idea that they were anything but God's intervention apparently never occurred to him. Nor did he consider his case exceptional; the waking vision and the dream were perfectly natural means for the transmission of divine commands, and through them everyone received some measure of relevation, according to his spiritual capacities. A thousand years later Richard of St. Victor presents essentially the same argument in a somewhat more abstract form when he calls visions 'Demonstrationes, quae Graeci vocant theophanias, id est divinas apparitiones, quae aliquando per signa sensibilibus similia invisibilia sunt.' (In *Apocalypsim Iohannis* 1, J. P. Migne, *Patrologia Latinia*, volume 196, column 687.)"

[18] A work of this type that covers developments in literature over many centuries has to be based on some theory of the historical relationships of what we now term the internal and external worlds. Since the study of the "History of Consciousness" is at present in a very fluid state, it is unlikely that any theory held today will remain long without modification, but it seems better to make explicit the thesis that one is following. While availing myself freely of the insights of Owen Barfield, *Saving the Appearances* (London, 1957) and Erich Neumann, *The Origins and History of Consciousness* (New York, 1962), I find the position most in harmony with

allegorists show an explicit awareness that the external forms in which these psychic forces clothe themselves are no more than emblematic of a higher reality; all serious allegorists clearly intuit the participation of their symbolic figures and *loci* in a higher reality. The images of the external world in which the autonomous powers of the psyche manifest themselves are usually traditional divinities or personifications, but from the fourteenth century we see a tendency for the allegorist to fuse the traditional images with those taken from his personal experience.

Medieval allegory itself frequently depicts a psychological process by which the spiritual forces are identified in the form of personifications, analysed in dialogue, and then either accepted or rejected for absorption into the personal psychic entity of those who participate in the spiritual processes the allegory embodies. In this respect, as in many others, medieval allegory refines and intellectualizes spiritual processes embodied in ancient myth and ritual.

---

my investigations to be that taken by Roger Hinks in *Myth and Allegory in Ancient Art* (London, 1939), especially his introduction: "Myth and Logic". Mr. Hinks outlines three principles I have generally found justified in experience:

> Unlike the physiological structure of the body, which is seen to be relatively stable and invariable over a wide area of time and space, the psychological structure of the mind exhibits rapid and remarkable changes within the limits of our observation. It would hardly be too much to say that the body has no "history", in the sense that the mind has a "history". (p. 93)

> . . . the intuitive and intellectual aspects of the mind have both co-existed . . . from the beginning, but . . . the intellect has gradually gained upon the imagination, without, however, being able to dispense with its services. (p. 5)

> The essential difference, then, between a mythical and a rational representation is not that the former is symbolic and the latter direct: both are symbolic—and in a sense both are also direct, since myth too after its fashion is self-explanatory and irreducible. The real difference lies in the ratio between the imagination and the intellect as the dominant modes of interpretation. . . . An absolutely mythical mode of thought and an absolutely logical mode of thought are abstract concepts: all concrete human thinking requires the collaboration of both myth and logic. . . . The so-called invention of logical thinking thus becomes merely the point at which the intellect, as it were, turns the scale at the expense of the imagination. (pp. 8–9)

NINE PROPOSITIONS

Since the argument of this book is somewhat complicated, I have reduced its essentials to nine propositions. These propositions do not receive equal stress in the book. The ninth, for example, is rather implied than demonstrated.

1. Medieval visionary allegory offers its readers participation in a process of psychic redemption closely resembling, though wider in scope than, modern psychotherapy. This process typically includes the phases of crisis, confession, comprehension and transformation.

2. The basic content and structural elements of such allegory consist largely of imagery derived from and constituting progressive developments of the imagery of classical and pre-classical religion and myth, as they are manifested in literature and art. Such imagery constitutes a dimension of allegory we should today term symbolic. The dominant or typical image is that of a goddess (*potentia*) in her grove, temple, or other sacred place (*locus*).

3. The other major element of such allegory is the dialogue, developed from its classical form to constitute a rational dimension of expression, through which the imagistic elements may be explicated and controlled, and the specific problems of the hero may be alleviated as they are viewed in the perspective of the total pattern, physical and spiritual, of human existence.

4. Medieval allegory as a mode of writing thus incorporates both rational and symbolic forms of statement. A third form of statement, intermediate between these two, is the purely allegorical. It will often take the form or constitute an aspect of a symbolical statement, but is distinguishable from it in that it more easily translates into rational terms, and makes a less profound effect.

5. The three modes which make up medieval allegory as a genre —dialogue, allegory proper, and symbolism—are distinguishable only in analysis and together constitute a total statement on all these levels of meaning, resulting in a form of communication of an extraordinary complexity and comprehensiveness.

6. From the structural point of view, medieval allegory functions primarily as a mode of analysis. The "seminal images", from which the allegorical vision typically derives, are analysed into rational, allegorical and symbolic elements, and the resultant visionary *loci* and *potentiae* are compared and contrasted in order to secure the reader's intellectual or emotional acceptance or rejection of these spiritual entities.

7. Fundamentally the quest of the visionary is for a principle of authority, usually manifested as a *potentia*, by which his life may be regulated. With the aid of the *potentia*, he finally achieves a psychic synthesis in which his emotional and irrational impulses, his intuitive understanding, and his rational principles are brought into harmony: in Freudian terms, id, ego, and superego are reconciled.

8. The major poets of medieval visionary allegory regard themselves as part of a cumulative tradition, in which each allegorist recapitulates, refines and develops the thought and imagery of his predecessors, exploring new dimensions of traditional topics, and, most important, attempting to integrate earlier thought and imagery pertaining to the topic into a coherent whole.

9. Allegory as a serious genre waned in the fifteenth century owing to the growing inability of allegorical poets to continue to achieve imaginative comprehension of the symbolical and mythical elements of the form. By the seventeenth century, a more strictly analytic approach to the phenomenal world made allegorizing seem intellectually trivial, and it was no longer possible to hold together in unity the three elements of dialogue, allegory and symbolism. The attenuated allegory of the eighteenth century, appealing to the reader on the allegorical level alone, bereft of serious psychotherapeutic purpose and of support from dialogue or symbolism, is responsible for the low opinion of allegory as a genre at the present time, as well as the lack of understanding of the complex and profound character of medieval visionary allegory.

2

The Seminal Images

BOETHIUS'S *Consolation of Philosophy* embodies in its opening a rhetorical effect so minor as to be almost unnoticeable unless one is aware of similar rhetorical patterns in other classical and medieval literature. In the first metrum of the poem the poet refers to his writing as inspired by his *lacerae . . . Camenae*, his wounded Muses. The reference is a brief one, seemingly a casual employment of the Muse as decorative, non-functional personification. In the prosa that follows, however, we encounter the Muses once more, this time as fully personified allegorical figures, who are driven away from the poet's bed by the lady Philosophy. Such development of inert but seminal personifications into allegorical *dramatis personae*, a common structural device in visionary allegory, might at first seem explicable in terms of Quintilian's dictum: *allegoriam facit continua metaphora* (*Inst.* IX.XII.46). While the relationship of rhetorical theory and poetic practice is never easy to determine with precision, we can assume that Quintilian's identification of allegory as continued metaphor is unlikely to have been of more than peripheral importance. His own examples of allegory (*Inst.* VIII.VI.14) consist of banal metaphors (of such *topoi* as the ship of state) continued for no more than a sentence. We can show, moreover, that the pattern of development of metaphor into allegory has much deeper roots in literature than in rhetoric, and hence we may assume that though Quintilian may have put a certain seal of rhetorical approval on the practice, he neither originated nor understood the bold and subtle structural patterns we are about to discuss.

It is noteworthy that the subjects of all the transformations of personification or metaphor into allegory that we encounter up to the twelfth century are goddesses or abstract personifications. As we look backwards into pre-Christian literature we find, as we might suspect, the origins of this rhetorical pattern in invocations of the gods. The action of Aeschylus's *Libation Bearers* is devoted almost entirely to invocation of the Eumenides, who, under extreme emotional and psychic tension, develop from mere inert "metaphors", or "seminal images", to a terrifying degree of active "personification" of the dark powers of vengeance. The peripeteia of the *Libation Bearers* consists in these dark forces emerging from the underworld in a much more objective form than Orestes expected.[1] The last play of the trilogy, *The Eumenides*, is taken up with the process by which the dark forces are placated, and coaxed underground once more. The final confrontation between the underworld passions and the forces of reason takes place on a hill of justice, where a wise and ancient goddess finds a rational and merciful solution to the problem of guilt. Nonetheless, Athene's decision also takes cognizance of the claims of the passions in an authoritative judgment that curiously anticipates later judgment scenes in Chaucer's *Parlement of Foules*, and Spenser's "Mutability Cantos".

Statius's *Thebaid* seems to have been the bridge by which these insights into the psychic world were carried over into medieval allegory. The starting-point for the *Thebaid's* psychological and rhetorical action is the searing description of Oedipus's emotional state after his discovery of Jocasta's true identity:

> Impia iam merita scrutatus lumina dextra
> merserat aeterna damnatum nocte pudorem
> Oedipodes longaque animam sub morte tenebat.
> illum indulgentem tenebris imaeque recessu
> sedis inaspectos caelo radiisque penates
> servantem tamen adsiduis circumvolat alis
> saeva dies animi, scelerumque in pectore Dirae.
>
> (I.46–52)

Now it was at this time that Oedipus had ravaged his guilty eyes with venge-ful hand, and had drowned the shame of his sin in eternal night, constraining his living soul in long abiding death. He yields himself to the shadows, the innermost recesses of his dwelling, shrines unseen of stars or sunlight, and yet with tireless wings the savage daylight of the mind hovers over him as he watches, and the crime-avenging Furies writhe within his breast.

[1] *Cf.* Philip Wheelwright, *The Burning Fountain* (Indiana, 1954), p. 243.

As Oedipus blinds himself, the distinctions between his internal and external worlds seem to become blurred. When he yields himself to the *tenebris imaeque recessu sedis*, the *inaspectos caelo radiisque penates*, we cannot say strictly whether these abodes are mental or physical, whether they pertain to his house or his soul.[2] In this state of extreme mental anguish, he is attacked unremittingly (*adsiduis alis*) by two forces: the *saeva dies*, the savage daylight—the horrifying enlightenment, and the *Dirae* (Furies).

What kind of reality can we ascribe to the *Dirae* at this point? Clearly they are so far no more than a name for, or inert personification of, the pangs of horror felt by Oedipus at the discovery of his incest. Their parallel position to the brilliant metaphor of the *saeva dies* makes this clear. But their reality will soon be of a much stronger order. In the following lines Oedipus addresses a prayer for vengeance on his sons (who have rejected him in his need) to the *di, sontes animas angustaque Tartara poenis qui regitis*, gods who would certainly include the *Dirae* even if we do not see here an exclusive reference to them. Of these gods, it is Tisiphone, the Fury especially associated with vengeance, to whom he particularly directs his appeal. Hearing his prayer, she stirs up enmity between his sons and thus sets in motion the whole tragic action of the poem. It is as if the prayer has transformed Tisiphone from a mere concept to an intensely active and powerful spiritual force independent of Oedipus's conscious control. Thus she subsequently intervenes at crucial points in the action, climactically and with decisive effect at the final and fatal encounter between the sons of Oedipus.

With the deaths of the brothers, Oedipus's curse is fulfilled, and the purposes for which Tisiphone was summoned are accomplished. But the physical death of the brothers has to be accompanied by a return of these anti-rational powers to the underworld, to their normal inert state of merely potential manifestation. The manner of their dismissal is closely parallel, rhetorically and psychologically, to that of their summoning. As soon as he hears about the deaths of his sons, the ancient monarch appears on the battlefield, repentant, and lamenting his part in stirring up their quarrel. In palliation of his responsibility, he cries:

[2] *Sedes* may refer both to the home and to the body as the home of soul; *penates* both to the inner sanctum of the home, and to the spirits of that sanctum.

furor illa et movit Erinys
et pater et genetrix et regna oculique cadentes;
nil ego:

(XI.619–21)

Madness and the Fury provoked these things, and my father and mother, my kingdom, my ruined eyes, but not I.

With her repudiation by Oedipus, Tisiphone sinks back into the collective anonymity of the *Dirae*, the Furies themselves becoming once again no more than a name for something in the mind, a mental abstraction capable of being made syntactically parallel with *furor*, a word used almost exclusively to denote a state of mind rather than an invocable and terrifying goddess. Thus Tisiphone does not appear again in the poem in her personified form, though Theseus, in his speech denouncing war against the impious Creon, raises the question of her reappearance: "quaenam ista novos induxit Erinys regnorum mores? . . . novus unde furor?" (XII. 590–3). (*Which of the Furies has caused this strange and immoral conduct among these powers? . . . Whence this new madness?*)

It is remarkable also that in the very speech in which Oedipus finally renounces the Furies, he asks, "estne sub hoc hominis clementia corde?" (XI.606) (*Is there clemency in this heart of man?*), since for much of the following book the poem is taken up by a description of the temple of *Clementia*, a goddess whose spirit, as expressed in the description of the temple, dominates the conclusion of the poem. *Pietas* also, the other main allegorical adversary of Tisiphone, appears several times in the form of an inert personification before she becomes a fully allegorized combatant.[3]

In the *Thebaid* Statius made a sustained attempt to represent and to analyse the mysterious emotional forces that underlie hatred and war. Such forces could not be adequately represented merely by naming them; only their manifestation in the form of mythological deities could effectively render their super-personal natures and their effects on the action. In the selection of Tisiphone as a representation of these powers he looks back to ancient Greek legends and beliefs, rather than around him to the beliefs of his sophisticated first-century audience.[4] He has taken certain liberties

[3] For *Pietas*, see *Thebaid* X. 597, 780; XI. 98, 458.
[4] C. S. Lewis has shown that the benevolent powers of Statius's moral world are, with the exception of Jupiter, almost always allegorical figures

with Tisiphone; she instigates crime as much as avenging it. But,
most important for our purposes, he anticipates medieval patterns
of allegory in his allegorical personification of states of mind under
conditions of extreme psychological stress.

Moving backwards in time, but forwards in terms of the development of this structural progression from mythical to rhetorical
patterns, let us look at Vergil's *Fama*, an allegorical figure who
influenced Statius's conception of Tisiphone.

> Extemplo Libyae magnas it Fama per urbes,
> Fama, malum qua non aliud velocius ullum;
> mobilitate viget virisque adquirit eundo;
> parva metu primo, mox sese attollit in auras
> ingrediturque solo et caput inter nubila condit.
> illam Terra parens, ira inritata deorum,
> extremam, ut perhibent, Coeo Enceladoque sororem
> progenuit, pedibus celerem et pernicibus alis,
> monstrum horrendum, ingens, cui quot sunt corpore plumae,
> tot vigiles oculi subter (mirabile dictu),
> tot linguae, totidem ora sonant, tot subrigit auris.
>
> (IV.173–83)

> *The loud report through Libyan cities goes.*
> *Fame, the great ill, from small beginnings grows—*
> *Swift from the first; and every moment brings*
> *New vigour to her flights, new pinions to her wings.*
> *Soon grows the pigmy to gigantic size;*
> *Her feet on earth, her forehead in the skies.*
> *Enraged against the gods, revengeful Earth*
> *Produced her, last of the Titanian birth:*
> *Swift is her walk, more swift her wingèd haste:*
> *A monstrous phantom, horrible and vast.*
> *As many plumes as raise her lofty flight;*
> *So many piercing eyes enlarge her sight;*

---

such as *Pietas* or *Clementia*, while the Olympian deities are only barely to
be distinguished from evil spirits. (See *Studies in Medieval and Renaissance
Literature* Cambridge, 1966, pp. 98–9.) Statius's poem marks a late
stage in the progressive reduction of the Olympian gods to the diabolic
status they sank to in the early Christian period. The general development
towards an ethical monotheism in the classical period expresses the lengthy
psychic struggle by which (in modern terms) miscellaneous intuitive impulses became subjected to some degree of control by the emergent
"superego".

Millions of opening mouths to fame belong,
And every mouth is furnished with a tongue;
(Dryden)

Here *Fama* gradually develops from a seminal personification to a fully fledged allegorical monster, a progression which constitutes a singularly bold and subtle literary effect. In line 173 *Fama* merely moves (*it*) while in the next line she is moving more swiftly, *velocius* (a word that already bestows more figurative force upon *it*); the next two lines describe her swift growth to a monstrous size, her head in the clouds. Then, in the lines immediately following, she becomes a solidly allegorical figure, one of the Titans, with a respectable mythological ancestry. Thus, throughout the opening lines of the passage, the development of *Fama* into a monster keeps exact pace with her equally explosive rhetorical progression from metaphor to allegorical figure, and the impetus of the progression reinforces the impetus of the rumour itself.

We are clearly concerned here with a pattern of expression that belongs more to the rhetorician than the student of myth, yet the connections between the subtleties of this passage in the *Aeneid* and the bald statements of the rhetoricians are almost certainly no more than accidental. Certainly it would be difficult for the most skilled interpreter to distinguish in rhetorical terms exactly how Vergil's allegory takes shape, though different stages of the development from metaphor into allegory can be distinguished. It is as if Vergil were searching out and exposing, in a rather fanciful manner, the original force behind the metaphor of "fama it". In this respect Vergil anticipates a method of rhetorical development much favoured by the medieval allegorist.[5] The specific type of figure chosen for development, a *potentia* suspended between the categories of abstract idea and goddess, will also be generally utilized. Nonetheless in some very important characteristics of Statius's or later medieval use of the pattern there is no anticipation in either Vergil or Quintilian. Most important, the medievals—and Statius —develop the inert seminal metaphor or personification into the imagery of a new world of allegorical vision.

[5] Previous writers on allegory do not appear to have paid much attention to the development of allegory from seminal images. An exception is Rosemond Tuve, who discerns this type of development in Deguilleville's *Pilgrimage of the Human Life*. See her *Allegorical Imagery* (Princeton, 1966), p. 199.

TECHNIQUES OF CONTROL

Moving forward to the fourth century and Prudentius's *Psychomachia*, we find Christianity and allegory, in the medieval sense, fully established. The *Psychomachia* lacks the subtlety and depth of the *Thebaid*, but embodies an important development of the psychic process we are tracing. The poem has a double preface. In the first we are treated to an allegorical interpretation of the life of Abraham as the life of the spirit. Just as Abraham was unable to have children before he overcame the *feroces . . . reges* who took Lot captive, so we are unable to produce fruits of the spirit until we have slaughtered the *portenta cordis servientis*, the monsters dwelling within the heart enslaved to sin. The second part of the preface consists of an address to Christ, whose assistance in identifying the contending forces in the soul is considerably emphasized. This part of the preface also has a reference to *portenta*, in the final lines before the poem proper opens:

> vincendi praesens ratio est, si comminus ipsas
> Virtutum facies et conluctantia contra
> viribus infestis liceat portenta notare.
>
> (18–20)

The right method to achieve victory is ours if we may mark face to face the very features of the Virtues, and the monsters that strive against them with hostile power.

This repetition brings out the distinction of method between the two parts of the preface. In the first the *portenta* are to be defeated in battle (*multa strage . . . vicerit*); in the second the *ratio vincendi* is no more than the discernment of these monsters. Thus the double preface gives us an insight into the double purpose of Prudentius's allegory, an insight of wide application which tells us something about allegorical methods in general. The correct analysis of the state of the soul is as important as the crushing of the evils one finds inhabiting it. Accordingly, it is not surprising to find that the terms *monstrum* and *portentum*, though they describe such vices as *Ira* and *Avaritia* in the battle itself, do not find a place in the concluding prayer of the poem. There the vices are simply referred to as *vitii*, for they now have been satisfactorily identified and labelled. (Even in the battle it is the deceit rather than the ferocity of the vices that presents the worst dangers.)

Clearly the *Psychomachia* has many similarities in structure to the *Thebaid*. The metaphor or personification is taken from the world of everyday speech and examined under the glass of allegory. Many passages in the opening prayer to Christ indicate the battle takes place within a mind under considerable stress: "quotiens turbatis sensibus intus seditio atque animam morborum rixa fatigat" (7–8). (*Whenever with thoughts in tumult rebellion arises within us and struggle with evil passions wears down the soul.*)

But it also embodies some significant developments in the use of allegory beyond the techniques of the *Thebaid*. Where Statius gives us Tisiphone and Megaera in all their pagan and primitive horror, Prudentius analyses the *portenta* into their rational components. His *ratio vincendi* is in fact to reduce the monsters to sins; in other words to separate the elements of sin from the elements of madness in the conception of the Furies, the rational from the irrational. With Christ's aid we may look at the monsters *comminus*, face to face, and recognize them for what they are. The two prefaces distinguish in fact the roles of priest and exorcist (or moralist and alienist). Nonetheless such analysis cannot be described as reducing the mental phenomena involved to purely rational terms. The appeal of the contending sins and virtues is directed to the fancy rather than the reason. To modern eyes, the complaint against Prudentius must be that his battle makes no appeal to our deeper imagination—the whole work gives an impression of trivial neatness. There is no Doubting Castle, no Valley of the Shadow of Death. But to look for such things in his work would be to misunderstand his whole purpose. His explicit aim is to rationalize away the ancient fears and divert the psychic energies against those aspects of the *portenta* that constitute sin.[6] His success in satisfying the psychic needs of his time can be judged by the enormous popularity of his work through the millennium to follow.[7]

Boethius's *Consolation of Philosophy* could be described as the intellectual's *Psychomachia*. The fanciful wars of Vice and Virtue

[6] Prudentius's own fervid descriptions of Proserpina and Trivia in the *Contra Orat. Symmachi* (357–78) give a convincing illustration of the type of monstrous horror that still infected the imagination of pagan and Christian alike at this period.

[7] See the "introduction historique" to Lavarenne's edition of the *Psychomachia* (Paris, 1933).

are transferred to the philosophical dialogue, the lofty arena of the rational mind. Nonetheless Boethius opens his dialogue with an allegorical treatment of the same question as that with which Prudentius opens his allegory: what psychic powers can be invoked to assist the embattled soul? The question is asked, moreover, in terms of the same allegorical technique, the development of a seminal personification into allegory, and under the same conditions of extreme mental stress.

The first metrum of the *Consolation* is confined to the expression of this disturbed mental state of the narrator; the lack of indications of time or space considerably intensifies the effect of disturbance which the passage creates. But the transition from confusion to ordered allegorical reality is being carefully prepared. The Muses that inspire the narrator's woeful verse in the metrum ("Ecce mihi lacerae dictant scribenda Camenae"—*Wounded Muses tell me what I have to write*) seems merely metaphorical, but with the arrival of the Lady Philosophy in the following prosa we find that they have become allegorical realities:

> Quae ubi poeticas Musas vidit
> nostro adsistentes toro fletibusque meis verba
> dictantes, commota paulisper ac torvis inflammata
> luminibus . . .

This lady, when she saw the Muses of poetry gathered around my bed and providing words to express my grief, became somewhat moved and aggravated to angry glances . . .

It does not take Philosophy long to get rid of these *poeticas Musas*, these *scenicas meretriculas*, as she calls them. Instead the prisoner is to be comforted by Philosophy's own Muses. ("Meisque eum Musis curandum sanandumque relinquite.") The Muses of Philosophy do indeed play an important part in the total work; for though they are never fully allegorized, Philosophy addresses much of her consolation to the narrator in the form of poetry. The movement from metaphor to allegory in the *Consolation* therefore represents a preliminary clarification of the narrator's mind, in which a type of consolation inappropriate to his condition is rejected when the true visionary authority manifests herself. In the next chapter we shall look more closely at Boethius's Lady Philosophy, who turns out to be an allegorical figure of an imaginative potency undreamed of by Statius or Prudentius, combining as she does the role of the personified virtue with the numinosity of the ancient pagan goddesses, and with the dialectical ability of the masters of the philosophical dialogue.

We have seen the first phase by which the invocation of the pagan deity, whether Olympian or chthonic, is transmuted into an important structural principle of medieval allegory. During later analyses, this structural pattern will be found recurring with remarkable persistency; in fact its most vivid re-emergence occurs over a thousand years later, in Spenser's "Mutability Cantos". Clearly this pattern was no vestigial survival from the mythopœic era; it represents a new more rational development of the same mental process—the identification, evocation, and full manifestation of the *potentiae*, the spiritual powers.

We may notice too that in the literature we have examined from Aeschylus to Prudentius, it is the chthonic anti-rational *potentiae* who are first invoked; their devastating irruptions can only be met by counter-invocations of the beneficent Olympian deities. While the direct invocation or irruption of the dark powers is naturally uncommon in the Christian era (though it occurs in the "Mutability Cantos"), the continuation of the pattern is nonetheless seen in the fact that all serious developments from seminal image to beneficent *potentia* are accomplished under extreme emotional tension, the result of oppression by what in earlier times would have been considered a manifestation of the dark powers. Thus it is always in answer to the hero's anguished call for help that the *potentiae* make their beneficent appearances.

3
Boethius

IT is commonly said that the philosophical dialogue was invented by Plato to represent the teaching methods of Socrates. Certainly it is a method of representing thought which has shown itself permanently attractive to the human mind. Where the *tractatus* presents results and conclusions already attained, the dialogue represents dramatically the process by which truth is elucidated. As Socrates says in the *Theaetetus* (190) "I speak of what I scarcely understand: but the soul when thinking appears to me to be just talking—asking questions of herself and answering them, affirming and denying", or the stranger in the *Sophist* (263) "what is called thought is the unuttered conversation of the soul within herself." Thus it is clear that the intimate connection between internal and external dialogue is recognized from the beginning. More generally, Ernst Cassirer connects Plato's creation of the dialogue form with Socrates' preoccupation with the nature of man, where previous philosophers had been more concerned with the nature of the physical universe. The question "What is man?" is answered indirectly, in the portrayal of a "creature who is constantly in search of himself—a creature who in every moment of his existence must examine and scrutinize the conditions of his existence."[1] If the dialogue achieves its effects by dramatizing a process in some sense internal, we should not be surprised to see it developing elements of allegory, by which the internal life of the mind is portrayed in a differing but compatible and complementary manner.

The typical roles in the classical dialogue are the questioners or provokers of discourse, and the discourser, who expresses the main positive ideas of the dialogue. For the discourser to be effective his authority must be respected; in a society such as Periclean

[1] *Essay on Man* (New York, 1944), pp. 19f.

Athens or among English-speaking peoples today such respect may prove difficult to obtain. Where the company are friends (as in the *Symposium*), the discourser may be chosen by succession or acclamation and his assumption of office may be preceded by modest and disarming professions of lack of competence. But in a period with greater respect for intellectual and spiritual hierarchy, the discourser may be given the status of some mythical figure, hero or god, or the personified embodiment of some allegorical principle, the figure we have previously termed the *potentia*.

There are several characteristics of the dialogue as a method of presenting thought which have been exploited in varying ways by those who have employed the form. For example, the discourser need not be (and in fact rarely is) identified with the author, which is advantageous when the latter wishes to present speculations rather than definite findings, or to incorporate at length views other than his own, or to present declarations too lofty or inspired to be appropriately attributed to the author himself. Further, it is the reader's natural inclination to sympathize or identify himself with the questioner, an identification which permits him to undergo by proxy a process of conversion to the discourser's point of view, his natural resistance to the teacher being vented in the objections of the questioner, and answered in the replies of the discourser. He may also, when the dialogue functions as a part of a wider process of spiritual enlightenment, participate not only in the questioner's acquisition of wisdom but in the acting out of the effects that the acquisition of this wisdom has on him.

Tracing further the history of the genre, we find that the dialogues of Cicero had little apparent effect on the medieval form. Cyril Bailey remarks of them: "The normal form of a philosophic dialogue of Cicero is the exposition and counter-exposition of the Stoic and Epicurean views, followed by a rather unconvincing Academic summary with a leaning to the Stoic side."[2] Here, the role of discourser is relatively weak; in general Cicero's characters seem insufficiently imbued with emotional commitment to any one point of view to achieve any substantial new intellectual or spiritual insight. The classical form of the dialogue is approaching its decadence. One may say that Cicero's bent was towards philosophizing rather than truth, or that the age was one of learned

[2] "Religion and Philosophy", *The Legacy of Rome* (Oxford, 1924), p. 252.

indecision; but his use of the dialogue was the reverse of the medievals'; in this point at least he had nothing to teach them.

With the *Consolation of Philosophy* of Boethius (*c.* 524) we find the medieval pattern fully established. In the intervening time patterns of thought have changed: the Christian revelation has occurred and largely under its pressure the shape of the dialogue has undergone radical alteration. So far as doctrine is concerned, the work has been called Platonic and Ciceronian. In situation, there is a clear resemblance to Plato's dialogue of the last hours of Socrates, the *Phaedo*. But the differences are more striking than the resemblances. In the *Phaedo* Socrates, the condemned one, is the discourser; he calms his anxious friends with a serenity which proceeds from a conviction that "no evil can happen to a good man either in life or after death". But the *Consolation* represents Boethius's struggle to attain such a belief, a struggle of a type infrequent in earlier literature. We never learn what Socrates experienced during the twenty-four hour trance he fell into on the Potidean campaign; he is portrayed complete and perfect in psychic stability, if not in comprehension of ultimate truth. The emphasis is on the development of the idea rather than of the individual.[3]

Socrates believed that knowledge of the good must inevitably lead to good actions. For him there was no substantial division between belief and action. But after the revelation had been accepted a new urgency appears; the seeker after truth becomes a struggler, an *agonistes*.[4] A man may now learn directly of good and be persuaded, alarmed or inspired into attempting to lead the good life; but the gap between knowledge and action grows frighteningly wide, and the processes of the mind described by Boethius become of general and urgent interest.

[3] Socrates at Potidea, see *Symposium* 220. For further discussion of the depiction of mental struggle in Greek literature, see Bruno Snell, *The Discovery of the Mind* (New York, 1960), pp. 101–3 (Aeschylus' Pelasgus) pp. 123–30 (Euripides' Medea and Phaedra), and pp. 132, 181, (Socrates).

[4] The *Agonistes*. I have not taken account of the fact that the later pagan world as well as the contemporaneous early Christians increasingly saw life as a moral struggle, because the general nature of this development does not greatly affect my argument. See C. S. Lewis, *The Allegory of Love* (London, 1936), p. 58.

For the history of the word *Agonistes*, see F. Michael Krouse, *Milton's Samson and the Christian Tradition* (Princeton, 1949), pp. 108–18. (The reader should be cautioned that Krouse's idea of "semantic amelioration" cuts across Owen Barfield's findings on the nature of language development as presented in *Poetic Diction* (London, 1951), pp. 77–85.)

LADY PHILOSOPHY

Thus the debate becomes increasingly internal and the dialogue a dramatized meditation. As C. S. Lewis has shown, with this turning inward of the mind comes a tendency towards allegory.[5] To term the *Consolation* allegorical merely because of the presence of an allegorical personification, Lady Philosophy, as discourser, would be an oversimplification. Dialogue has a constant tendency to utilize personifications. Even in Plato's dialogues we frequently find characters with names which hint at their point of view or manner of debating.[6] But the allegorization of the classical dialogue manifested in the *Consolation* embodies profound changes not only in new assumptions about the revealed and stable nature of truth, but still more in the emphasis on the spiritual character of the process by which it is acquired. These new emphases are largely expressed in the persona of Lady Philosophy which, while seemingly simple and straightforward to rational understanding, embodies considerable complexity in its conceptual, historical and psychological dimensions.

Let us turn first to her conceptual significance. A good starting point is Professor Highet's remark in *The Classical Tradition*:[7]

Although *The Consolation of Philosophy* is a synthesis of the arguments of many other philosophers and the images of many other poets, it is much more than a collection of echoes. The noble character and able mind of Boethius himself are manifest all through it; and they make it a unity.

[5] See *The Allegory of Love*, pp. 6off. The relation between allegory and the dialogue seems largely to have escaped the attention of literary historians. Charles Muscatine, however, in his article "The Emergence of Psychological Allegory in Old French Romance", (*PMLA*, December 1953, pp. 1160–82), examines the depiction of the emotional crises of the heroes and heroines of Old French Romances in terms of dialogue between allegorized voices of reason and the affections. Muscatine relates the tendency of the meditative monologue to break into dialogue to other tendencies towards self-analysis in contemporary writers on mysticism such as Richard of St. Victor, in the moralistic tradition of Seneca, Marcus Aurelius and Augustine, and in the passionate monologues of Ovidian heroines in crisis.

[6] See the discusson in *The Portable Plato* edited by Scott Buchanan (New York, 1948), pp. 13, 34ff.

[7] *The Classical Tradition* (New York, 1957) p. 42.

Philosophia then, it is easy to suppose, is not intended to be the mouthpiece for any new ideas of Boethius's. Nor, however, is she quite "what philosophy says" to a man in his terrible situation. For she speaks as if she reminds rather than instructs, and what she says is clearly in some sense already present in Boethius's mind. In fact the use of the allegorical figure of *Philosophy* enables him to maintain a valuable ambiguity with a precision and absence of strain that would be impossible in a direct exposition. For an idea remembered is not the same thing as an idea as first encountered, but again it is not quite a part of one's own mind. The dialogue represents the movement of a doctrine, a body of ideas, from a position almost external to the mind, to a point where the ideas have become part of the equipment, even the constitution, of the mind itself. Since there is no question of discovering or presenting anything original—truth is known, and to be absorbed and lived— the dramatic tension is highest in the beginning when the conflict between the mind and truth is sharpest, and dies away as the mind and truth become part of each other.[8] The same pattern, the same movement of ideas into the mind, may be discerned when one looks at the *Consolation* as a religious rather than an intellectual work. In this respect the struggle is to believe inwardly and manifest in actions what is confessed on one's lips, a battle close to the centre of the religious life. Lady Philosophy is in this aspect the better self, the higher mood, something which seems as if it ought to be part

[8] *Truth is known.* With the rise of Christianity the intellectual problem becomes relatively diminished and the moral problem receives greater emphasis. The sin of *odium theologicum*, unintelligible as it would be to Plato, now becomes a possibility. How the change affected contemporaries may be illustrated from Justin Martyr's "Dialogue with Trypho a Jew" (in *The Ante-Nicene Fathers* I, p. 195):

> What philosophy is, however, and the reason why it has been sent down to men, have escaped the observation of most; for there would be neither Platonists, nor Stoics, nor Peripatetics, nor Theoretics, nor Pythagoreans, since this knowledge [is] one. . . .

The educated pagan tended to accept the same doctrine, but in a fashion that would bring no difficulties about divergencies in opinion between philosophical sects:

> Therefore, I say, let no one divide philosophy into many kinds or cut it up into many parts, or rather let no one make it out to be plural instead of one. For even as truth is one, so too philosophy is one. But it is not surprising that we travel to it now by one road, now by another.

This is from Julian's *Oration* VI, "To the Uneducated Cynics".

of us and yet remains agonizingly separate unless it can be absorbed through earnest struggle.

But Lady Philosophy as an allegorical figure also appeals to the mind on less abstract levels than these, as a more imaginative and figurative conception. As a Christian *imago* she is not only analogous to but even an aspect of the personified figure of the Church, the *Mater Ecclesia* or the Hagia Sophia. It is certainly possible that Boethius was acquainted with the similar role played by the Lady Ecclesia as *potentia* of the second-century Christian allegorical dialogue, *The Vision of Hermas*, although this work was apparently little known in the western Church.[9] In terms of her relationship to the prisoner, the contemporary or medieval reader would be reminded of his early catechetical instruction in the basic precepts of his faith. From the earliest periods the Churches had employed the catechism as the principal method of instruction; and the opening questions of Philosophy to the prisoner have something of the blunt demand for definite answers on fundamentals which seems to have distinguished Christian catechism in all periods.[10] Such a catechetical relationship is highly appropriate to the spiritual situation in which the poet depicts himself, for he has suffered an abrupt reversal of fortune and now finds himself in a

[9] See H. LeClercq's article "Hermas" in *La Dictionnaire d'Archéologie Chrétienne et de Liturgie* Volume 6, pp. 2270–80.

[10] The verb *catechisare* seems to have had at the time of Augustine both the general sense of to instruct (candidates for baptism) and to instruct by asking questions. The ambiguity reflects the practice for, as Augustine makes clear in the *De Rudibus Catechisandis* (chapter XIII), a good catechist might teach by direct discourse or by asking questions. In particular he recommends questioning the educated candidates (chapter VIII). The situation of the *Consolation* perhaps also reflects the rather overpowering formal questioning of the candidates for the admission to the catechumenate or to baptism, a time of reckoning. Thus the educated man must humble himself before revealed truth. Rudolf Hirzel says, rather unsympathetically, "Die dialogische Form, die, bei ihrem ersten Hervortreten in der Geschichte, der Kritik der Meinungen und der Befreiung des Geistes gedient hatte, war in den Katechismen das Gefäss des rohesten Dogmatismus geworden. Daher besiegelt die Katechismenliteratur das Ende des antiken Dialogs" (*Der Dialog* II, Leipzig, 1895, pp. 364*f*). Hirzel thus recognizes the connection between the dialogue and the catechism, but is less than just to the aims and achievements of the medieval dialogue.

See also the Rev. Joseph P. Christopher's edition of St. Augustine, *The First Catechetical Instruction* (Westminster, Maryland, 1946), *Dictionnaire de Théologie Catholique* II (1897), and *Disputationes puerorum per interrogationes et responsiones* (J. P. Migne, *Patrologia Latina*, volume 101, 1097) which gives an example of the "question and answer" method in action.

dungeon, verging on despair at the extremity of ill fortune he has suffered. The prisoner achieves his salvation by putting himself in the hands of the catechist, by humbling himself—becoming a little child again—and learning to see the injustices done to him in a new light. Thus a close parallel arises between the situation of the prisoner and the experience of conversion in general. The world becomes a microcosmic prison from which release is only to be expected in death; man's business in it is to prepare himself for that end under the shadow of that end. Ripeness is all.

Lady Philosophy has also a role as a pagan *imago*, the archetype as it manifests itself in a local historical setting. If one looks back to the classical dialogue, one finds (apart possibly from Socrates' *Diotima*) no real antecedents of these wise female discoursers. But it is not at all likely that *Philosophia* is an independent archetype. A clue to the source of the *imago* in earlier literature may be found in the fact that the Romans made little distinction in certain circumstances between abstractions, particularly feminine abstractions, and deities. They found no difficulties in raising temples to *Virtus*, *Pax* or *Clementia*. Among the many roles of *Philosophia* is that of abstraction-goddess, the contemporary shape of the *potentia animae*. This role of *Philosophia* had been played in the past by such goddesses as Thetis in the *Iliad*, Pallas Athene in the *Odyssey*, or Isis in the *Metamorphoses* of Apuleius.[11] These goddesses manifest themselves to the heroes under their care in order to help them with advice rather than by direct intervention in their difficulties, and to send them on their way encouraged and emboldened. In medieval allegory the pagan goddesses are replaced by figures more acceptable to the Christian imagination (such as Nature, Reason or Holychurch), but while their intellectual stance undergoes appropriate modification their basic psychic function remains remarkably constant.

Our survey of the *imago* manifested in Lady Philosophy, confined as it was to the question of sources and influence, did not of

---

[11] See the discussion in E. R. Curtius, *European Literature and the Latin Middle Ages* (New York, 1953) pp. 101*ff*. Diotima may be seen as a figure transitional between the goddess and the mistress of discourse, if we accept the connection Bachofen makes between her and the Mantinean Aphrodite (*Das Mutterrecht*, Basel, 1897, chapters 143, 146). Apuleius's Isis is discussed further below, p. 61. *Cf.* also Hans Jauss, "Form und Auffassung der Allegorie in der Tradition der Psychomachia", in *Medium Aevum Vivum, Festschrift für Walther Bulst* (Heidelberg, 1960), especially p. 186.

course account for the extreme literary and iconographic vitality of the visionary *potentia* in the classical and medieval periods, their persistent "archetypal" appeal. Evidence adduced in previous chapters suggests that the mysterious figure of the *potentia* has been a vivid imaginative reality in the literature, art and dreams of western man up to the period of the Reformation. We need to consider here some further evidence relevant to the ultra-historic dimensions of Lady Philosophy, in order to comprehend something of the psychic tendencies that shape the general characteristics of the historical *imago*.

What seems specifically archetypal in the *Consolation?* The hero is in a state of doubt and perplexity. To him comes the vision of a venerable figure, a *potentia*, invested with proper authority, who, after prolonged discussion, resolves his difficulties—a sequence that did not escape the ancient classifiers of dreams. Macrobius says: "We call a dream oracular in which a parent, or a pious or revered man, or a priest, or even a god clearly reveals what will or will not transpire, and what action to take or to avoid."[12] His immediate text being the *Somnium Scipionis*, he has in mind the relatively practical nature of the prophecy of Africanus to his grandson.

Modern theorists are more specific. C. G. Jung writes of the archetype of the "old man" as it appears in dreams and fairy tales:

The old man always appears when the hero is in a hopeless and desperate situation from which only profound reflection or a lucky idea . . . can extricate him. But since, for internal and external reasons, the hero cannot accomplish this himself, the knowledge needed to compensate the deficiency comes in the form of a personified thought; that is in the shape of this sagacious and helpful old man. . . . Often the old man in the fairy tales asks questions like who? why? whence? whither? for the purpose of inducing self-reflection and mobilizing the moral forces, . . . the intervention of the old man would seem to be indispensable since the conscious will of itself is hardly ever capable of uniting the personality to the point where it acquires this extraordinary power to succeed.[13]

[12] *Commentary on the Dream of Scipio* translated by William Stahl (New York, 1952), p. 90.
[13] "The Phenomenology of the Spirit in Fairy Tales", in *Psyche and Symbol* (New York, 1958), pp. 73, 75. *Cf.* Anchises' appearance to the troubled Aeneas in *Aeneid* V.721*ff.* Philip Damon ("Twelfth Century Latin Vision Poetry", *diss.*, University of California, 1952, p. 13) says: "The formal structure of the medieval waking vision's manifest content

Jung's analysis comes remarkably close to the circumstances of the *Consolation* in many respects—the desperate situation, the need for reflection, the appearance of a *potentia* who asks catechetical questions in order to support the inadequate conscious will of the hero. But there are striking differences. The assistance of the old man is apparently restricted to practical rather than spiritual advice, although symbolic interpretation of the tale can readily distinguish spiritual aspects of his advice. Secondly, the *potentia* in medieval allegory is almost invariably feminine, possibly an important psychic distinction or possibly a mere reflection of the fact that Latin and Greek grammar attribute femininity to most abstract concepts. It seems difficult, however, to believe that grammar controls concepts; rather one would expect that the quality of the concept is reflected in grammatical gender.[14]

We should finally touch upon those characteristics of Lady Philosophy which might be considered particularly allegorical in the popular, almost the derogatory sense of the word—the mystic characters marked upon her dress to allegorize the ascent from "action" to "contemplation", and the tear in the dress which signifies the dissensions of the different schools of philosophy. Superficially these decorations seem too trivial for the dignity of the work, products of the late Latin fascination with trite personifications. The details, however, are few and not badly chosen; the ladder foreshadows the spiritual ascent the prisoner has to make (nor is the superficial significance of the ascent from *practica* to *theoretica* inappropriate[15]), and the torn garment gives an echo of the miser-

appears to have been strongly conditioned by the stereotyping influence that Lincoln [*The Dream in Primitive Cultures*, London, 1935] has noted, and to conform in general to two principle 'culture-patterns' derived from the medieval cultural context. The first of these motifs is the apparition of an impressive and awe-inspiring figure, perhaps a deceased spiritual superior or respected friend, an unknown person of obvious authority, or a member of the celestial hierarchy." See also R. J. Werblowsky, *Joseph Caro Lawyer and Mystic* (Oxford, 1962), pp. 75–6, 78, 165, for an account of the angels called *maggidim*, the *potentiae* of Cabbalistic mysticism of the late medieval period. "They are a kind of hypostasis of the moral and spiritual level reached by man, and they come as near to a 'psychological' theory of revelation as the 'projecting' thought of sixteenth-century kabbalism could formulate" (p. 78).

[14] *Cf.* Ernst Cassirer's citation of H. Usener's *Götternamen* (Bonn, 1896), p. 375, in *Language and Myth* (New York, 1946), pp. 42–3.

[15] *Theoretica* here implies much more than comprehension of the theoretical aspects of philosophy. As Werner Jaeger points out: "The

able state of his mind, which is due to his failure to pull himself together mentally and to make use of and coordinate the truths he has received in the past. If truth is one and in part knowable, the dissensions of jarring sects are a parallel on the philosophical plane to confusion in the mind of the individual.

There remains the one action of *Philosophia* not directed specifically to her patient. On her first appearance she sweeps away from the prisoner's bedside the "poetic" Muses, who have been unsuccessfully attempting to console him. The reflection of the low estimate of poetry in Platonic and Patristic theory is obvious enough,[16] but since a good deal of the *Consolation* is composed in stirring poetry it is clear that we cannot equate the Muses here with inspiration (in the sense of the *furor poeticus* of the *Ion*); the distinction is more likely to be Jerome's, between the beautiful fictions of the pagan poets and the profound speculations of the searchers for truth.[17] But whatever particular interpretation we make of these Muses, the important thing for the future is that we have a rejection (expressed in allegorical terms) of something which can be thought of either as a way of interpreting experience or, at the same time, as a mode of expression—we lack a phrase to express a concept quite clear in its allegorical presentation—and this implies a comparison of two or more of these modes of interpreting and

---

theoria of Greek philosophy was deeply and inherently connected with Greek art and Greek poetry; for it embodied not only rational thought, the element which we think of first, but also (as the name implies) vision, which apprehends every object as a whole, which sees the *idea* in everything—namely the visible pattern" (*Paidea*, New York, 1965, p. xxi). For Aristotle, *theoria* is a state of Godlike contemplation, the supreme state of existence possible for man. (*Metaphysics* 1072b, pp. 14–29.) Medieval visionary poetry in general might be regarded as a means to the attainment of *theoria*.

[16] See Curtius, *op. cit.*, pp. 39ff.

[17] *Philosophia* dismissing the *poeticas musas* ends "meisque eum Musis curandum senandumque relinquite". The decline in the esteem of the Muses in later antiquity is noticed by Curtius (pp. 232ff.), and evidence for a similar frivolity of treatment in late classical art is found in Roger Hinks' *Myth and Allegory in Ancient Art* (London, 1939), p. 103f. Of particular relevance to our interpretation of *Philosophia*'s role is his description of a miniature in the sixth-century Rossano Gospels of St. Mark receiving dictation from a tall, venerable, austerely-clothed lady. "She is Holy Wisdom, Sophia: her ancestresses are the Muses, but how great is the difference; whereas they suggested, whispered, or enticed, she utters stern commands—the difference between the pagan and the Christian attitude to inspiration could hardly be more marked" (p. 105).

expressing experience. The Christian, attempting to shape his life so as to fit one pattern, naturally makes such comparisons and rejections in the search for the mental states most productive of harmony with God, and the authorities, *potentiae*, most likely to assist him in that search. Thus allegory becomes a clear and natural way of expressing such processes.[18]

COSMIC ALIENATION

In medieval visionary allegory the emotional tone of the situation is frequently conveyed by images of landscape and setting. In the *Consolation* the use of such imagery is relatively undeveloped, the visionary authority, *Philosophia*, constituting the main unifying image. The locale of the dialogue is the prison cell throughout, an appropriate setting for one imprisoned psychologically by the trauma of his worldly downfall, and which both physically and psychically separates him from the normal processes of the universe.

While there is little development of the imagery of the locale itself, a series of metric interludes provides a poetic commentary—using chiefly cosmic imagery—on the intellectual and spiritual progress of the dialogue between Philosophy and the prisoner, and shows the chief phases by which the dissociated soul of the prisoner is gradually brought back into harmony with the cosmic order. In book I, this dissociation is clearly depicted in the second metrum, where Philosophy complains that

> He that did bravely comprehend in verse,
> The various spheres and wandering course of stars, . . .
> Revealing every secret of Nature's laws
> Now having lost the glory of mental light
> Lies with his neck weighed down by heavy chains.

In the fifth metrum the cosmological argument is stated in the prisoner's terms when he laments that the rule of the lord of the

[18] Curtius, *op. cit.*, discusses a topos of rejection (p. 235) in connection with Christian treatment of the Muses.

heavens ("stelliferi conditor orbis"), who governs all cosmological phenomena, does not extend also to the deeds of man, which are directed by slippery Fortune. Thus Lady Philosophy's task is to restore the prisoner's links to the higher world of the cosmos and release him from the spiritual chains that bind him to the earth. In the second, third and fourth books the majority of the metra are devoted to Philosophy's denunciations of those who pursue fame, wealth, power, and other untrustworthy gifts of Fortune, but the negative tone of these poems is relieved by celebration of the operations of cosmic harmony and order, as in the great hymns to cosmic love (II.viii) and natural law (III.ii). In poetic and imaginative terms the crisis of the work occurs in the magnificent "O qui perpetua . . ." (III.ix) in which the motions of the soul are analysed in terms of the imagery of the chariots from Plato's *Laws*, and for the first time Lady Philosophy prays explicitly that the soul may be raised on high to the throne of the Father. In the following metra this theme is consolidated, receiving final expression in metrum IV.i, where the triumphant ascent to the spheres of the soul-chariot is described in detail, and the heavenly kingdom identified as the soul's native land.

This dimension of poetic cosmology in the *Consolation* was to prove highly influential in later vision poetry. It no doubt influenced the choice of the figure of Nature as visionary *potentia* and passed on to medieval allegorists a demonstration of soul healing through contemplation of the cosmic and natural orders, a method which we can trace back to the *Timaeus* (90c) in seminal form, but which seems to have been given its first extensive embodiment in this work.

ALLEGORY AND SYMBOLISM

Is it fair to say that the *Consolation* embodies a form of allegory which functions as a mode of thought? C. S. Lewis made a general objection to our thinking of allegory in this way. In the *Allegory of Love* he wrote:

There is nothing "mystical" or mysterious about medieval allegory; the poets know quite clearly what they are about and are well aware that the figures they represent to us are fictions. Symbolism is a mode of thought, but allegory is a mode of expression. It belongs to the form of poetry more than to its content . . . (p. 48)

Lewis cautioned us that the medieval allegorist does not feel himself "to be reaching after some transcendental reality which the forms of discursive thought cannot contain." (p. 47) His distinction between the different modes of allegory and symbolism is based on a clear definition of their different functions. In the case of allegory you "start with an immaterial fact, such as the passions which you actually experience, and can then invent *visibilia* to express them. . . ." But if

our passions, being immaterial, can be copied by material inventions, then it is possible that our material world in its turn is the copy of an invisible world. . . . The attempt to read that something else through its sensible imitations, to see the archtype in the copy, is what I mean by symbolism. . . . The allegorist leaves the given—his own passions—to talk of that which is confessedly less real, which is a fiction. The symbolist leaves the given to find that which is more real. (pp. 44–45)

I believe that the distinctions made here are fundamental to the understanding of the relationship between allegory and symbolism; but there are two objections which could be advanced against the theory as it stands, which leads me to suggest a modification in it.

The first objection is to the description of the allegorical figure as in a sense fictional, "less real" than the passions it represents. (It is this, I think, that makes allegory in Lewis's view a mode of expression rather than one of thought.) The word "real" is a dangerous one. Since the activities of the psyche are never perfectly representable by any mode of human expression, it is difficult to agree that allegory is less real than any other means of conceptualizing psychic experience, merely because the allegorist personifies the terms of his analysis. The onset of a mood of anger, for example, is a mysterious event. It is easy to forget that the mood's existence in the mind and in its external effects is primary to its recognition and identification on the part of the person who experiences it. In fact, the cool statement: "I am in a state of anger" can hardly be made by one who is thoroughly possessed by anger; the utterance of such a statement is itself an act of rational self-control. Thus the very naming of the concept "anger" begins to modify the experience which it is desired to express. The process by which anger or other strong emotions possess a man can thus be more accurately depicted by allegory, which, with its unbroken connections with the pre-allegorical mythical or "symbolic" mode of depicting psychic events, is able to draw freely on such figures as Tisiphone or Venus. Since these names do not rationalize the psychic experience by directly identifying or asserting the primacy of the abstract quality of the *potentia* involved, they can better preserve the reality of the mysterious experiences of the internal world. These figures of pagan myth are of course supplemented in allegory by personifications whose basic mode of action is similar to that of the mythical figures with whom they mingle freely but whose naming circumscribes and controls their actions. Allegorical personifications are considered less interesting today as literary figures than pagan gods, but we should recall that the naming of these powers was more than a mere literary technique,—rather a means of achieving the essential identification and control of forces which might otherwise overwhelm the rational governance of the mind. The personification, therefore, far from being judged a poor relative of the normal modern means of expressing states of mind through abstract rational analysis, should rather be considered an important and effective transitional form between the mythopœic use of pagan divinities and the modern use of abstract terms to denote mental states. Medieval personifications often embody the power of the underlying mythical figures along with the prosaic accuracy of abstract terms, thus achieving appropriate expression of both the dynamic and the analytic aspects of the psyche.

I make these qualifications with the greater confidence since Lewis himself implied these arguments when in the same work he wrote concerning the mind of the Roman Christian: "For such a man allegory will be no frigid form. It is idle to tell him that something with which he has been at death-grips for the last twenty-four hours is an 'abstraction'." Of the *Romance of the Rose* he warns us not to be misled by modern allegory into thinking "that in turning to Guillaume de Lorris we are retreating from the real world into the shadowy world of abstractions."[19]

[19] *Cf*. Lewis, p. 61 and n., p. 115. The argument appears to be a development of the influential Coleridgean statement, referred to in a footnote to page 11. See Morton W. Bloomfield, "A Grammatical Approach to Personification Allegory", *Modern Philology* 61 (February 1963), p. 169, for some criticisms of Lewis's position from a linguistic standpoint.

The second and related qualification is thus that in much medieval allegorical writing, allegory and symbolism (in Lewis's sense) are in fact inextricably mixed. Lady Philosophy, as we have seen, represents an element in an intellectual process, and is at the same time an embodiment of the universal figure of the lady of wise aspect who comes to us in our troubles, surely a copy of something in the invisible world, a symbol. Moreover, in these instances, as perhaps in all successful allegory, we perceive the two sets of representations as one; they can only be separated by analysis.

It seems appropriate to suggest a modification in Lewis's theory. Allegory is a method of representing states of mind, symbolism of representing an invisible world, of which our experience is but the copy of an archetype. But the distinction between the two modes is not so absolute. In some sense all deities do reside in the human breast.[20] The invisible world exists in the human mind (or perhaps on its deeper levels the human mind exists in the invisible world). Symbolism represents these deeper levels, whereas allegory, as in Lewis's definition, represents the more conscious processes. But the mind itself functions simultaneously and indivisibly on all these levels, and medieval allegory as a genre at its best represents all these levels. Therefore, it is not only a mode of expression but, more fundamentally, a mode of thought. Poets have been able to employ allegory to express, develop and make judgments on concepts unattainable in their time and circumstances by discursive thought, and attainable now only through the prisms of analysis. Allegory blurs distinctions when they would be unnecessary and distracting, and permits what is discursively complex to be represented symbolically with a directness and a unity of impression that suggests an underlying unity in the "reality" of the invisible world. Such was the form created by Boethius and such the underlying structure of the work which was to satisfy the spiritual needs of poets and thinkers of Christendom for some eight hundred years.

[20] Blake, *Marriage of Heaven and Hell*.

4

Alan's Vision of Nature

#

SOME six and a half centuries separate Alan of Lille's *Complaint of Nature* from the *Consolation of Philosophy*, but the later work seems to be not merely influenced by the earlier but even a conscious attempt to produce something in the same genre. It is in fact one of the closest imitations of Boethius's work, particularly with regard to allegorical technique; Petrarch's *Secretum* is closer to the *Consolation* in subject, but Petrarch passes over the subtleties of the allegory, which made so great an impression on Alan.

The literary reputation of the *Doctor Universalis* has waned since the days when he was respected as a major authority by allegorical poets of the stature of Jean de Meun, Dante and Chaucer. While there is doubtless much in Alan's work that is now permanently beyond our imaginative sympathies, yet a deeper understanding of his intentions and achievements in the *Complaint of Nature* may give us greater respect for this seemingly arid work. The *Complaint* has sometimes in the past been dismissed as a tract against sodomites, somewhat infected in its tone and style by the material with which it concerns itself.[1] My contention is that it is best understood as a visionary allegory whose purpose, in accordance with the ancient tradition of the genre, is to offer to its reader participation in the process of psychic and spiritual integration it embodies, and thus follows Boethius's *Consolation* not only in respect of its techniques but also its basic purposes and functions.

---

[1] It has been shown by R. H. Green (what a careful reading can hardly fail to reveal) that the sexual vices castigated in the first Prosa are, in the context of the whole work, to be thought of as a symbol, or perhaps one might better say a synecdoche of a wider corruption. ("Alan of Lille's *De Planctu Naturae*", *Speculum* 31 October, 1956.) Since Alan's intention seems in part to be the construction of a poetic fable as a representation of the accepted philosophical truth that all vices are contrary to nature, his statement of the case will be most effective poetically and rhetorically if he places the vices most notoriously unnatural in the forefront of his work.

THE COMING OF LADY NATURE

The opening of the *Complaint*, like that of the *Consolation*, depicts the poet not yet caught up in the visionary experience, but undergoing the intense mental turmoil that seems the inevitable prelude to it. Once more, too, the gulf that separates us from the world of visionary allegory is bridged by the development of a seminal personification into a full allegorical figure.[2] Indeed Alan's opening seems a direct imitation of the *Consolation*. The first metrum of each introduces a personification who will play an important role in the following prosa, the *Camenae* (Muses) in the *Consolation* answering to the personifications of Nature in the *Complaint* (see above p. 29). But Alan's use of this method of introducing the visionary experience is much more extensive and complex; he presents, moreover, the seminal personification of nature in a manner that recalls the invocations of the goddess from which this method of obtaining a vision must ultimately derive:

> Musa rogat, dolor ipse jubet, Natura precatur
> Ut donem flendo flebile carmen eis.
> Heu! quod Naturae successit gratia morum
> Forma, pudicitiae norma, pudoris amor!
> Flet Natura, . . .   (II, p. 429)[3]

The Muse requests, Sorrow itself demands, Nature implores that in my weeping I give them a tearful song. Alas! Where have the grace of Nature, the beauty of character and morals, the standards of virtuous chastity, the love of modesty disappeared? Nature weeps . . .

And as in the *Consolation*, the anguished cry of the poet is answered by an immediate vision of the goddess. Yet these preliminary

[2] The fact that Johan Huizinga called the "transition from the rather obscene opening strophes to the appearance of Nature . . . as flat and clumsy as it is sudden" suggests that the development of seminal image into allegory is not obvious to the modern reader. I hope the analysis presented here will permit a modification of Huizinga's judgment ("Über die Verknüpfung des Poetischen mit dem Theologischen bei Alanus de Insulis", *Mededeelingen der Kon. Akad. van Wetenschappen* 74B, chapter 6, Amsterdam, 1932, p. 17).

[3] All quotations for the text of the *Complaint* are from Thomas Wright, *The Anglo-Latin Satirical Poets of the Twelfth Century* II (London, 1872). The *Patrologia Latina* volume 210 may also be consulted.

references to Nature in the form of seminal personifications constitute only one aspect of the connections between the psychological
situation depicted in the opening lines and her manifestation as a
full allegorical *potentia*.[4]

During the course of his denunciations of unnatural sexual
behaviour in the first metrum, the poet suddenly turns on a new
tack to sing the praises of natural sexuality. Women's beauty is
immeasurably superior to man's, arguably divine, he asserts. Why
then is she spurned?

> Virginis in labiis cur basia tanta quiescunt,
>   Cum reditus in eis sumere nemo velit?
> Quae mihi pressa semel mellirent oscular succo,
>   Quae mellita darent mellis in ore favum.
> Spiritus exiret ad basia, deditus ori
>   Totus, et in labiis luderet ipse sibi.
> Ut dum sic moriar, in me defunctus, in illa
>   Felici vita perfruar, alter ego.
>
> (II, p. 430)

*Why do so many kisses slumber unawakened on the lips of our maidens? Is
there no one who wishes to profit from them? If such lips were once pressed on
mine, they would sweeten them with sweet flavours, would give a honeycomb
of sweetness to the mouth. The spirit would expire in kisses, totally yielded
through the mouth, and itself would play on the lips. And while I thus
expire, dead to myself, I should in her, as a second self, live the happiest of
lives.*

This outburst of woman-worship seems not unexpected or un-
worthy of a contemporary of Marie de Champagne or for that
matter Bernard of Clairvaux, but here woman is neither a saint nor
a courtly *midons*; this is a straightforward though very fervent
depiction of the natural sexual desire a woman may appropriately
stimulate. In itself this powerful evocation of heterosexual eroticism
reflects the normal opinion current among poets of the Chartrian
school; it also, so far as the *Complaint* itself is concerned, introduces

---

[4] Alan also goes beyond Boethius in having a number of seminal
images and themes. Venus and Genius, other actors in the main allegory,
also appear as limited seminal personifications in the first metrum; the
themes of the perversions of classical heroes and heroines, and of grammatical forms, will also reappear in a more coherent and orderly exposition
in the allegorical vision itself.

one of the main themes of the work, anticipating in particular the at times surprisingly erotic descriptions of Nature herself, in her subsequent manifestation as *potentia*, her feminine charms often receiving emphasis in a manner strongly reminiscent of the description of woman in the preceding metrum: "Labia, modico tumore surgentia, Veneris tyrones invitabant ad oscula." (*The lips, rising in a slight swell, invite Venus's freshmen to a kiss.*) It is not in fact until the end of this description that we learn: "non Dyonea clavis hujus sigillum reseraverat castitatis." (II, p. 432) (*The key of Venus had not unlocked the seal of her chastity.*) Not that there has been any suggestion in the preceding metrum that virginity is necessarily pale and unawakened. A line such as "Virginis in labiis cur basia tanta quiescunt . . .?" suggests that Alan is equating the neglect of nubile girls with man's neglect of nature in general.

A little later, at the opening of the third prosa, Alan describes how he was so overcome at the appearance of *Natura* that he lost control of his senses.

Quam postquam mihi diu cognatam loci proximitate prospexi, in faciem decidens, mentis stupore vulneratus, et totus in extasis alienatione sepultus, sensumque incarceratis virtutibus, nec vivens nec moriens inter utrumque neuter laborabam. Quem virgo amicabiliter erigens, pedes ebrios sustentantium manuum confortabat solatio, meque suis innectendo amplexibus, meaque ora pudicis osculis dulcorando, mellifluique sermonis medicamine a stuporis morbo curavit infirmum.

(II, p. 449)

. . . falling on my face, I was assaulted by stupor of mind and totally immersed in an ecstatic trance; my mental powers imprisoned, I wavered between life and death. But the maiden kindly raised me up, sustaining my unsteady steps with her comforting arms. Then, gathering me into her embrace and sweetening my lips with chaste kisses, she brought me out of my stupor and healed my infirmity by the mellifluous balm of her speech.

Here the effect on the poet of Lady Nature (described as "virgo") seems remarkably close to that predicated of the "virgines" of the first metrum. In particular her kisses, though described as modest, seem to have a similarly powerful effect of healing and consolation.

To this point, therefore, the relationship of the poet and the Lady Nature has developed in a surprisingly erotic fashion. It almost seems as if her feminine charms were being put forward as a rival attraction to the perverse temptations deplored in the first metrum. But such an interpretation, we immediately learn thereafter, would constitute a misapprehension: in his "extasis alienatione" the dreamer has failed to recognize his old nurse, his "nutrix familiare", (the term Boethius first uses in description of his relationship with Lady Philosophy.) In the course of the ensuing prosa, Nature defines at some length her role in the hierarchical scheme of things, as intermediary between God and man in the work of creation, and takes a cool look at the necessary but subordinate role of the sexual impulses in the divine scheme, intended as they are to be under the control of *magnanimitas* and *sapientia*. ("Renes vero, tanquam suburbia, cupidinariis voluptatibus partem corporis largiuntur extremam, quae magnanimitatis obviare non audentes imperio, ejus obtemperant voluntati."—II, p. 453—*Now the loins, like suburbs of the city, comprise an outer area of the body given over to the pleasures of love, but these parts, not daring to oppose the orders of Magnanimity, conform to her will.*) This speech of Nature's is successful in clearing up the dreamer's initial confusion in a number of different ways:

Cum per haec verba mihi Natura naturae suae faciem develaret, suaque admonitione quasi clave praeambula cognitionis suae mihi januam reseraret, a meae mentis confinio stuporis evaporat nubecula. (II, p. 457)

When by these words Nature had unveiled the appearance of her nature to me, and by her admonition as if with a key had (going on before) unlocked the door of her acquaintance for me, the little cloud of insensibility evaporated from the confines of my mind.

In such a conscious artist as Alan the repetition of the phrasing of "non Dyonea clavis hujus sigillum reseraverat castitatis," can only be intentional; the "key" to the right use of Nature is not sexual but rational "cognitio".

The negative aspect of this theme of the correct attitude to Nature emerges in the following (fourth) prosa in Nature's account of the tearing of her robe.

Tunc ego "Miror cur quaedam tuae tunicae portiones, quae texturae matrimonii deberent esse confines, in ea parte suae conjunctionis patiantur divortia, in qua hominis imaginem picturae repraesentant insomnia." Tunc illa: "Jam ex praelibatis potes elicere quid mystice figuret scissurae figurata parenthesis. Cum enim, ut praedicimus, plerique homines in suam matrem vitiorum armentur injuriis, inde inter se et ipsam maximum chaos dissentionis firmantes, in me violentas manus violenter injiciunt, et mea sibi particulatim vestimenta diripiunt, et quam reverentiae deberent honore vestire, me vestibus orphanatam, quantum in ipsis est, cogunt meretricialiter lupanare. (II, p. 467)

Then I said, "I wonder that certain parts of your tunic which ought to be woven like the texture of matrimony, suffer divorce in just that place where the visions of art have depicted the image of man." She replied, "Now from what we have previously mentioned, you can deduce what the gap made by this rent allegorically represents, for, as we said, many men have armed themselves against their mother with the assaults of the vices, creating the greatest chaos between themselves and her. They lay violent hands upon me, ripping up my clothes piece by piece, and although they should clothe me in honour and reverence, they force me, so far as they can, stripped of my clothing, to prostitute myself as a whore."

This motive of the torn robe is also to be found in the *Consolation*, but here its function is considerably expanded. *Natura* has already been identified poetically and symbolically with woman as object of reverence and affection, and now those who follow unnatural sexual practices are represented as committing a rape upon *Natura*, their mother, in breach of the normal or marriage relationship. The sin is here exposed as being against nature, against the loving reverence naturally due to one's mother and to all women, a sin obviously associated with the unnatural sexual behaviour described in the first metrum.

Developing the hint he found in the *Consolation*, Alan thus establishes connections between the chaotic states of feeling depicted in the first metrum and the figure of *Natura*, with the effect not only of increasing our sense of her function in the work but also, as it were, carrying out an analysis in allegorical terms of the states of mind depicted in the metrum—a type of analysis which will appear frequently in later medieval allegory.[5] In the first phases of the *Complaint*, however, this process of analysis raises more questions than it solves. Unnatural sexual relationships have been analysed and condemned, but the status of normal erotic relationships remains somewhat unclear at the outset, though they

[5] Such analysis appears most notably in the *Commedia*, the *Pearl* and (parodistically) in the fifth dialogue of the *De Amore* of Andreas Capellanus. See the appropriate discussions below.

will later constitute the topic of an earnest debate, which we shall take up in the final section of this chapter. But first we should consider the allegorical and symbolic dimensions of Lady Nature in greater depth, especially with regard to a further question raised in this discussion, the strange notion of sexual attraction between man and *potentia*.

COSMOS AND MORALITY

This section examines more extensively Alan's presentation of the figure of Nature in the *Complaint*, in terms of both the positive traditional influences that helped to form the complex and in many ways surprising conception he presents, and also the negative influences of certain views of the natural world that he undoubtedly knew of and seems to have been concerned with.

Nature's role as mistress of discourse differs significantly from that of Lady Philosophy in the *Consolation*. Where the latter represents (among much else) the mode of thinking by which the dreamer's problems will find solution, Lady Nature corresponds rather to the principle on which the resolution is to be based. The first step in establishing her in this role we have already traced in the daring synecdoche in which she becomes, for a time at least, the object of the dreamer's erotic admiration. But beyond this she is made the representation of the normal processes of earthly phenomena, with which is associated, in a manner somewhat mysterious to the modern reader, the principles of the moral life.

In three successive prosae Nature is described in respect of, first, the totality of created things as depicted on her clothing and adornments, second, the stimulating effect of her arrival on the welcoming world, and third, her function as intermediary between God and man. Her diadem depicts the properties and revolutions of the astral bodies; her robe, an assembly of the birds of the air; her mantle, the beasts of the sea; her tunic, land animals; her shoes, plants and flowers. Each item in the catalogue of creation is described lovingly and individually in respect of its distinguishing quality. Though they seemed to be there in reality, says Alan, they were only there allegorically, as if the whole natural world, "the great globe itself", was but an allegory of its *creatrix* (II, p. 439). In the next prosa we learn of the general rejoicing of the elements at her arrival. The stars shine in the heavens though it is still daytime; air and sea fall into a cheerful calm. The fishes rejoice, nymphs offer gifts, the earth blooms forth in flowers and blossoms as if it were spring; animals indulge in the pleasures of copulation.[6] The process of healing thus starts with the contemplation of the created universe, the *naturata*, ascending by degrees to the higher reality of the *naturans*, the creating power.[7] The assumption underlying the extraordinarily long and elaborate description of Nature in

[6] *Cf.* Gautier de Chatillon, *Alexandreis* X (*Patrologia Latina* volume 209, column 563) for a similar, though more tersely expressed, account of the effect of the arrival of Nature on her creatures.

[7] I am using *naturans* and *naturata* with, perhaps, slight anachronism, but these terms seem highly appropriate for the distinction Alan evidently wishes to emphasize in the *Complaint*—that between Nature as a creating or regulating power, and the totality of created things. A good Chartrian realist, Alan gives primary emphasis to the *naturans*; his description of her garments is rounded off with the admission: "Haec vestium ornamenta, quamvis plenis suae splendiditatis flammarent ardoribus, eorundem tamen splendor sub puellaris decoris sidere patiebatur eclipsim." (*Although these ornaments of her garments flashed with the brilliance of their splendour, yet the splendour suffered eclipse by the star of the maiden's own beauty.*) The distinction is an obvious one in an age of "realistic" perception. So far as the *imago* of *Natura naturans* is concerned, there is ample precedent in the great poetic celebration of the powers of Nature in the third book of the *Consolation* (metrum II), as well as hints in Statius (*Thebaid* XI.466 and XII.56) and Claudian (*The Consulship of Stilicho* II.424). The separation of creation and procreatress, ultimately as old as the conception of the nature goddesses themselves, is supported intellectually and philosophically by Chalcidius's *Commentarius* on the *Timaeus*, where Natura, Fortuna and Casus are described as subordinate powers, "ministras . . . potestates", to the Triune Deity (edited by J. H. Waszink, London, 1962, c. 188), as well as by that other favourite of the Chartrian school, Scotus Eriugena, in respect of his analysis of one aspect of nature into "that which both creates and is created" (*De Divisione Naturae* I, I). Alan himself refers in passing to the mediating role of Nature in the work of creation (*Contra Hereticos* I, XL, *Patrologia Latina* volume 210, column 545D) in the words: "Cum ergo Deus, mediante Natura, res procreaturus esset, propter peccatum Adae noluit mutare legem naturae." His treatment of nature in his philosophico-theological *Distinctiones* (*Summa Quot Modis, Patrologia Latina* volume 210, column 871) does not touch upon Nature as an active force, and seems less relevant. (But for a different view see G. Raynaud de Lage, *Alain de Lille*, Paris, 1951, pp. 65–6). See also the brief but learned appendix "Natura, Nature, and Kind" in J. A. W. Bennett's *The Parlement of Foules* (Oxford, 1957) and M-D Chenu, *La Théologie au Douzième Siècle* (Paris, 1957) pp. 30–34. Edgar Knowlton's "The Goddess Nature in Early Periods", *Journal of English and Germanic Philology* 19, pp. 224–53) contains a particularly detailed survey of her manifestations.

these various roles appears to be that the controlled contemplation of earthly phenomena, and the *potentiae* responsible for their creation and ordering, is in itself an act productive of calming and healing effects, an implication to be found extensively elsewhere in later medieval allegory, as we shall see. Such contemplation also permits the object of the dreamer's (or patient's) obsessive attention to be viewed in relation to the general processes of the universe, and thus to be reduced to its natural proportions within his mental perspective. Alan's depiction of the raiment of Nature being torn only in one location (where man himself is depicted), demonstrates this principle in a graphic image (II, p. 467).

While the association of the order of nature and the harmony of the psychic life can thus be argued to have an immediately perceptible fitness, and can perhaps also be demonstrated in practical experience, we should also be able to show that such an association is widespread generally in western culture, since an arbitrary linking of these apparently very distinct feelings would hardly achieve the effect Alan desired. Though one scholar has seen Alan as original in the linkage of cosmos and morality,[8] in fact we can trace such an association as far back as evidence exists; it seems almost an essential element in the *imago* of the Nature Goddess. The ancient Mesopotamian goddess Innana-Ishtar was a guardian of morals as well as the source of all living creatures. R. M. Cornford interprets the concepts of Nature (Phusis) and Custom (Nomos) as "not merely harmonious, but identical" in the Greek consciousness of the pre-philosophic period. In Greek thought generally we find the conception *cosmos* denoting the moral as well as the physical order of things.[9]

[8] *Cf.* Raynaud de Lage, pp. 10, 73–4.

[9] See Hastings's *Encyclopaedia of Religion and Ethics*, art. "Ishtar", IV, 8. For Cornford: see *From Religion to Philosophy* (New York, 1957), especially pp. 73–4. For an illuminating discussion of Greek and Gnostic views of the *cosmos* see Hans Jonas, *The Gnostic Religion* (Boston, 1963) chapter 10. Nature's description of her activities in the fourth Prosa of the *Complaint* includes a statement that might have been applied with virtually no modification to the Greek *Moira*: "The sea is joined to the land by firm ties of friendship through the interposition of my mediation, not daring to violate the sacrament of faith sworn to its sister, and it fears to overstep the determined limits of its extension into the dwellings of the land." (Wright II, p. 461). *Cf.* Cornford, pp. 12–19, for the parallel role of *Moira*, who is never anthropomorphized, however, to the degree of Alan's Nature. *Cf.* also the figure of Nature as depicted by Gautier de Chatillon (or Lille) in the tenth book of the *Alexandreis* (*loc. cit.*). She is

These relatively simple relationships apart, the association of the cosmic figure with moral law takes more complex forms, the tracing of which may help us to establish more precisely the mythical and archetypal dimensions of Alan's Lady Nature. I have used the term "archetypal" here advisedly, since Alan's Lady Nature constitutes a rare though by no means unique case where some of the main features of the *potentia* have to be explained as direct manifestations of an archetype, unmediated by the formal influence of traditional *imagines*. In the *Complaint*, as in similar cases of an apparent direct manifestation of an archetype unmediated by the form of an *imago*, we shall see that the psychological pressures behind its appearance could hardly have manifested themselves in a form conventional to the culture in question. Nonetheless, we shall also find that the archetypal characteristics of Lady Nature are themselves subtly affected by the spiritual and psychological environment of the period.

Certain elements in the figure of Nature are clearly imagistic, accessible to Alan in the cultural traditions available to him. So far as the purely cosmological aspect of "great creating nature" is concerned, she derives most directly from Bernardus's *Physis* of the *De Universitate Mundi*, though the identification of the cosmological figure with the moral governess is, of course, no fresh development on the part of Alan himself, as we have seen. What is new in Alan is that she does not merely represent or teach a system of abstract ideals, but becomes something more Messianic and Christlike in conception: one who comes down to earth, rebukes and pleads with sinners, suffers ignominy at the hands of wicked men, as the torn robe bears witness, and finally brings peace to the anguished soul. In this respect, therefore, the chief mediating *imago* is Boethius's Lady Philosophy, but here informed by an intensified emotional pressure basically Christian in character.

There also appears to be an important negative influence behind Alan's extended description of *Natura* and the *naturata* as depicted on her vestments of creation. Cathars, at least as Alan understood them when he wrote his *Contra Hereticos*, believed that the material

---

the procreatress of all things from the original *hyle* or matter, gives orders to all created things that they should not pass their bounds, and is shocked at the unnatural acts of Alexander, who passes the bounds natural to man. This work was probably influenced by Bernard and in its turn influenced John of Hanville, though the dating and order of these works seem not beyond question.

world is evil and the creation of the devil (I. II, III; in *Patrologia Latina* volume 210). The heresy creates the orthodoxy, and we can understand why Alan finds it particularly opportune to emphasize the *naturata* and its relationship to the creative principle and the Creator; if morality can be linked to the cosmos, as was the traditional view, it is not too difficult to see the *naturata* affirming the moral order. Alan indeed makes an explicit connection when he shows, by an ingenious adaptation of an allegorical symbolism of the *De Consolatione*, that it is man alone who has torn *Natura*'s apparel and spoiled the harmony of creation. It may well be that those who reduce *Natura* to prostitution and infamy represented to Alan, on one level of interpretation, the Cathars, since they imputed a diabolic origin to the natural world, repudiated normal sexual relationships, and (in the opinion of the orthodox at least) indulged in unnatural orgies. Alan, who was associated with Montpellier during part of his career, certainly must have been acquainted with Cathars at first hand; it has even been asserted that he served on the papal inquisition.[10] At all events the excommunication pronounced by Genius against the unnatural would be equally appropriate as a treatment for heretics. It is only necessary to add here that the dispute between Alan and the Cathars has also its archetypal dimensions, which can more conveniently be treated later.

Let us now turn to those aspects of *Natura* that seem to be best interpretable in archetypal terms. Very percipiently, Ernst Curtius has remarked on one of the manifestations of Lady Nature in twelfth-century allegories: "Here, then, as through an open sluice, the fertility cult of the earliest ages flows once again into the speculation

---

[10] The most recent authoritative study of Alan's life is in Marie D'Alverny, *Alain de Lille, Textes Inédites* (Paris, 1965); see especially pp. 14–16. For Cathar orgies see Steven Runciman, *The Medieval Manichee* (New York, 1961) pp. 120–1, 175–7; Runciman perhaps makes too much of the rather limited evidence available. The intersexual behaviour deplored in the *Complaint* may have been inspired by either orgiastic developments of, or misunderstandings of, the Cathar doctrine of the bi-sexuality of the Deity and the attribution of the creation of sex to the Devil, a doctrine which we can certainly associate with the Cathar treatment of women as equals. See Gottfried Koch, "Die Frau im mittelalter-lichen Katharismus. . . ." *Studi Medievali* (Spoleto, 1964) pp. 741–74, especially pp. 76off. Alan appears as Inquisitor in Runciman, p. 151. The relevance of Alan's anti-Catharistic polemic to the *Complaint* has also been noted by Professor Aldo Scaglione in *Nature and Love in the Late Middle Ages* (Berkeley, 1963), pp. 34–5.

of the Christian West."[11] Curtius does not make clear, however, whether he considers the sudden intensification of interest in this figure to be the result of the "uprush" of some archetype from the collective unconscious, or whether he believes there is some significant continuity of tradition between the ancient goddesses and our twelfth-century figures. James in *The Cult of the Mother Goddess* (New York, 1959), suggests that specific influences of the Phrygian mother-goddesses on the Christian conceptions of the *Mater Ecclesia* and the Madonna were not important after the fifth century, though inevitably the Christian "mother-goddesses" would be a receptacle for some of the same emotions directed towards their pagan predecessors.

Nonetheless, whether we regard it as archetypal or imagistic in character, some impressive evidence can be adduced to show the closeness of Alan's conception of *Natura* to pagan conceptions of the Mesopotamian Ishtar, the mother-goddess *par excellence*. Though subject to a higher 'creator' god, Anu, Ishtar presided over vegetation and animals, over the sexual functions and over the institutions of marriage, birth and death. She gave revelations in dreams and visions, exorcised demons, as well as being a governor and corrector of morals, opposed to all disorder. She too weeps over the sins and misfortunes of mankind, and is a compassionate goddess who loves righteousness. *Natura* is celebrated by Alan to a greater or lesser extent in all these aspects, and scarcely in any others. But one can go beyond this catalogue of common attributes and show a common situation. The opening metrum of the *Complaint* gives us a picture of a world which has lost or broken away from *Natura* as a force or guide towards right conduct, and is restored to health by the return of her presence and influence. Let us look backwards.

In the Sumerian poem concerning the descent of Ishtar to the underworld, Papsukkal, "vizier of the great gods", informs Sin, his father:

Since Ishtar has gone down to the Land of No Return,
The bull springs not upon the cow, the ass impregnates not the jenny,

---

[11] *European Literature and the Latin Middle Ages* (New York, 1953), p. 123. Denis de Rougemont's account of "The Psychical Revolution of the Twelfth Century" (*Love in the Western World*, New York, 1956, pp. 107–10) gives an interesting interpretation of this development.

In the street the man impregnates not the maiden.
The man lay down in his (own) chamber,
The maiden lay down on her side.[12]

Similarly, we learn in the Hittite poem of the anger of the god
Telepinus:

Telepinus went and lost himself in the steppe; fatigue overcame him.
So grain (and) spelt thrive no longer. So cattle, sheep and man no longer
breed. And even those with young cannot bring them forth.

The vegetation dried up; the trees dried up and would bring forth
no fresh shoots . . .[13]

We see the same motive appearing in the better known Greek
legend of the desolation of the earth during the period of Demeter's
mourning for the loss of Persephone beneath the earth; here the
absence of the goddess is in part provoked by a sense of moral
outrage.[14] It is not difficult to understand how in a primitive community scarcity of food would lead to a decline in vigour, particularly sexual vigour, and a slackening of the general current of life
within the community. Cause and effect, not being clearly distinguished, might be described as the result of the absence of a god,
and the Telepinus poem actually contains the magical formulas for
inducing him to return.

As scarcity and the fear of scarcity grow more remote, the
absence of the god may represent a spiritual malaise in society or
the individual. For example, in the late and sophisticated story of
Cupid and Psyche in Apuleius's *Metamorphoses*, a seagull reports
to Venus that as a result of her and Cupid's neglect of the earth,

per hoc non voluptas ulla, non gratia, non lepos,
sed incompta et agrestia et horrida cuncta sint,
non nuptiae coniugales, non amicitiae sociales,
non liberum caritates, sed enormis eluvies et
squalentium foederum insuave fastidium.

(Loeb edn., p. 240)

---

[12] *Ancient Near Eastern Texts* edited by James B. Pritchard (Princeton,
1958), p. 108.
[13] Pritchard, p. 126.
[14] *Hesiod: The Homeric Hymns and Homerica* (London, 1920), p. 311.

Because of this, pleasure, grace, and wit have disappeared and everything has become disordered, crude and boorish. Marital duties, love of friends, and care and affection for children no longer exist, and apart from every other kind of enormity we find that these neglected relationships arouse nothing but a disgusting squeamishness.

So a surprisingly consistent pattern emerges of a goddess of sexuality or fertility causing confusion and disorder by her absence and afterwards returning in order to put matters to rights. Alan's *Natura* certainly fits this pattern quite neatly and to this extent Curtius's dictum can be said to be well justified. But here the world has fallen into a state of sexual confusion not through a god or goddess being temporarily unavailable to look after her charges on earth, but because men have deliberately turned away from her. Consequently, when *Natura* returns, her mere appearance is not enough to put things to rights; persuasion and threat are necessary to bring men to their senses. The goddess no longer operates on man's unconscious instincts alone but also on his rational functions and his conscience. The difference marks very clearly the distinction between allegory and myth.

The basic difference between Alan and the Cathars, or more generally between Christian and Gnostic, can also be analysed archetypally in terms of the differing attitudes they developed towards the major *imago* they inherited from earlier civilizations, the Great Mother of the Gods. While the Christian tradition took over the elements of the Virgin Mother and the maternal Nature goddess in Ishtar, it rejected that aspect of the goddess concerned with "perverse" or unnatural, non-fertile sexuality.[15] The Gnostic treatment of the basic figure was almost diametrically a reversal of this. Rejecting the world of nature, Gnostic thinkers accepted only the most spiritual and intellectual elements of the Great Mother figure, which they personified and apprehended in the form of the Sophia.[16] Her fall into the material world (the fusion of Sophia and Natura figures) was for the Gnostics *the* Fall, the primary act of the universal tragedy. The whole duty of the Gnostics therefore lay in assisting the Sophia, or at least her earthly emanation, to free herself from the world of matter. In other words, they wished to

[15] Hastings, *loc. cit.* ("Ishtar") IV, 4.
[16] Wilhelm Bousset has made an interesting study of the relationship of the Gnostic Sophia to earlier concepts of the *Magna Mater*. See *Encyclopaedia Britannica* (11th edn.) XII, pp. 155*ff.*

sunder the archetype of the Universal Female in just the place where the Christians, affirming the unity of moral and cosmological orders, wished to see it most entirely fused.

Contrariwise, it was the task of Alan to make a split in the original archetype of the Mother Goddess exactly where the Cathars would preserve a wholeness, that is, between the two aspects of Venus, the chaste Venus of marriage and the Venus *pandemos*, the instigator of excessive and irregular sex, to vindicate the one and to repudiate the other. Thus the opening note of the *Complaint*: "Venus contra Venerem pugnans", and the elaborate distinction between the two sons of Venus, the legitimate Cupid and the bastard and dissolute Jocus. Ancient history makes amply clear the effect of the Great Mother on those who come excessively under her domination without having achieved the sundering of the archetype: they suffer the very emasculation against which Alan protests at such length in the *Complaint*. The effeminacy and castration of the priesthoods of Ishtar, Cybele, and the Dea Syria, expressive of the archetypal sacrifice of Attis, demonstrate the peril.[17] Much myth and legend in the western tradition manifests attempts to control the archetype in this fashion of forcing an analytic distinction between its favourable and unfavourable aspects. We can see such attempts reflected in the Judgment of Paris, in the *Aeneid*, especially Book IV, and with particular clarity in Apuleius's *Metamorphoses*, where the hero first falls under the domination of the lustful Venus but is rescued from his state of degraded animality by the pure and noble goddess Isis. That the contrast is intentional and well-controlled in Apuleius appears in the fact that the careless and vindictive Venus of the Psyche story boasts herself "rerum naturae prisca parens, en elementorum origo initialis" (*Metamorphoses*, Loeb edn., p. 188),

---

[17] A Freudian interpreter of the *Complaint* would have no difficulty in detecting the suppressed castration symbolism of the lines describing the need to "moderate" the assaults of Cupid: "Non enim originalem Cupidinis naturam in honestate redarguo, si circumscribatur frenis modestiae, si habenis temperantiae castigetur, si non geminae excursionis limites deputatos evadat, vel in nimium tumorem ejus calor ebulliat; sed si ejus scintilla in flammam evaserit, vel ipsius fonticulus in torrentem excreverit, excrementi luxuries *amputationis falcem* expostulat, exuberationis tumor solatium medicamenti desiderat; quoniam omnis excessus temperatae mediocritatis incessum disturbat, et abundantiae morbidantis inflatio quasi in quaedam apostemata vitiorum exuberat." (Wright, II, pp. 474–5).

while in the final revelation of Isis, the true goddess, merciful and solicitous, in an echo of Venus' language is described as "rerum naturae parens, elementorum omnium domina, saeculorum progenies initialis, . . ." (p. 544). Just as previously we saw that allegory provides a method of mastering the dark and sinister forces of the psyche by confrontation, naming, and analysis, so here ambiguous powers, such as that represented by Venus, are controlled by a similar method. Let us note, however, that the analysis is carried on predominantly in terms of imagery rather than abstract conceptions, for the aim is not merely an appeal to the intellect but to the whole mind, to feelings, emotions, instincts, all faculties that can be more directly affected by imagery. The aim of the poet is to effect not only an intellectual understanding but primarily a psychic amelioration.

It cannot be too firmly emphasized that these Gnostic or Christian allegories were by no means fanciful fairy tales, but expressions of the fundamental psychic organization of those that accepted them. In Christian society the female was fully accepted in the roles of virgin or mother, but she was never permitted to attain to the higher spiritual authority of the priesthood nor the higher intellectual authority which admission to Latin culture and the universities might bring. Among the Gnostics, on the other hand, the female was highly acceptable in the role of the virgin, not so much specifically because of the freedom from sexuality involved, but rather because of the Gnostic repudiation of the whole material world. Thus if the Gnostic woman was not one of the perfected ones she would be better employed, it seems, in infertile or perverse sexual behaviour than in the normal sexual functions which replenish the material world. But she was admitted freely to high spiritual authority and was enrolled among the perfected ones, the priestly cast of the Gnostics, on a basis of equality with men. In other words, she might pattern herself on the type of the Sophia but not on Lady Nature or the Virgin Mother. The Gnostics were in fact notorious in refusing to honour the Virgin Mary, treating her as a mere woman, or alternatively interpreting her as a purely immaterial being.[18]

The characteristic features of the figure of Nature in the *Complaint* thus appear to be a compound of many diverse influences, some positive, some negative, some conscious, some unconscious,

[18] See Koch, pp. 772*ff.*, Runciman, p. 149.

all intimately connected. Doubtless we shall never know the exact process by which, for example, Alan utilized the ancient motif of the "Absence of the Goddess" to reflect on social mores, most probably Catharistic, of the twelfth century. Nor, more generally, can we be sure to what extent he consciously emphasized the link between cosmos and morality as a vindication of an enduring tradition as well as of an eternal truth. The most we can do is indicate the broad shape and limits of the intellectual and intuitive milieu in which his vision functions, and express, so far as we can, the imaginative potential of his images. But whatever conscious intention one sees in Alan's portrayal of Nature, it may be agreed that, like the Lady Philosophy, she constitutes a figure that does more than merely express the poet's pre-formed thought; she is rather a figure prior to, though also subject to, the poet's intellectual understanding and commentary. She is an image that demonstrates the way in which visionary allegory functions, not only as a mode of expression but, more fundamentally, as a mode of thought and feeling.

THE THERAPEUTIC DIALOGUE

Considered as dialogue in the Boethian or classical tradition, the *Complaint of Nature* appears to be a degenerate descendant of the earlier forms. The dreamer is in complete agreement with Lady Nature, it appears, even before she arrives on the scene. His position is thus weakened from provoker of discourse to that of recorder. He asks a few helpful questions but hardly stimulates conversation by intellectual resistance to Nature's arguments. Indeed, the *Complaint* has been criticized as containing no true dialogue, but rather a series of expositions.[19] Such an appraisal, however, would do less than justice to Alan's achievements. The classical form of the dialogue is here developing further in the direction already taken by Boethius, from a method of arriving at new intellectual truths to a psychodrama directed to the intuitive and emotional functions and shaped so as to promote the healing and reintegration of a mind in spiritual turmoil. As we have seen, the therapeutic process consists in part of a sustained contempla-

[19] See Raynaud De Lage, p. III.

tion of the basic images of the natural universe, and of the *potentia*, Lady Nature, who orders and maintains that universe. Since these images are intended to appeal to the reader's intuitive perceptions, we have so far had to concern ourselves with the difficult task of reconstructing something of the imaginative potential of his work.

It remains therefore to describe the function of the dialogue in relation to the principal aims of the work. If we were to think of the *Complaint* as directed chiefly to the reason as such, we should immediately have to condemn it (as some critics indeed have) as absurdly prolix and repetitious. The very concept of unnatural behaviour implies a condemnation. Why elaborate? The *Complaint*, however, represents the necessarily lengthy process by which the controlling action of the rational mind asserts itself over disordered emotions, constituting a *psychomachia* fought out not in terms of Prudentius's gory Vergilianesque melées but with the subtler weapons of the dialectic. Nonetheless, the basic psychological strategy by which the evil forces are overcome remains the same as those we have already discerned in Prudentius. They must be identified, analysed, confronted by forces of healing, and finally repudiated or destroyed.

The stages by which these disordered impulses are brought under control will not be hard to distinguish. We are first presented with a picture of the mind in a state of feverish obsession with the seeming universality of unnatural sexual behaviour. (At this stage, it is irrelevant whether we think of these abnormalities as located generally in external society, specifically among the Cathars, or within the poet's or reader's own psyche; the *Complaint*, as a work of healing, can be read in any of these ways.[20]) The poet's obsession distorts every subject that comes within his view: classical legends, for example, and even grammatical constructions, gender and agreement, are pressed into service to reflect the pervading

---

[20] The *Complaint* may be interpreted with some justification as the record of a personal internal struggle of the type of the *Consolation*. This would give a special relevance to certain borrowings from Boethius: the preliminary anguish, and the consternation of the narrator at the first sight of *Natura*. The constant tension and alternation between pictures of vice and virtue and the final resolution of excommunication thus become aspects of an internal struggle within the poet's mind, and the consequent relief of the decision enables the poet to awake refreshed. The innerness of the vision and the introduction of *Natura* into the matter thus become relevant to the type of mental event depicted.

abnormality. Psychologically as well as rhetorically his world has been turned upside down.

With the coming of the Lady Nature, the first stage of the work of healing begins. We turn from fevered verse to relatively cool prose. At this point, there is no direct confrontation of good and evil; instead the mind is steadied by the long contemplation of the ordered universe. This induces a very different mood in the dreamer, and he breaks out into the hymn of praise "O Dei proles", celebrating the glories of Lady Nature's rule over earth and the heavens, at the conclusion of which he is sufficiently calmed to be able to ask the lady why she weeps; his anguish has now been successfully projected on to the *potentia*.

Her answer seems to cover at first very much the same ground as the opening metrum. Sexual abuses are depicted once more in terms of classical instances, from Helen to Narcissus, and in terms of grammatical and rhetorical indecorum. But this time sexual perversity is related to a wider scheme of things; we for the first time learn that man is the only creature of Nature's to break her laws and to behave unnaturally, so that his abnormalities appear in their proper context of the general order of the universe as described over the preceding three prosas—they no longer obsessively dominate his total outlook. Furthermore, Nature, responding to the dreamer's questions, explains at length what made man fall under the spell of sensuality, lose rational control over himself, and defy her laws. Her answer incorporates a creative and Platonistic use of myth for the purpose of analysis: Venus has fallen into lassitude, has failed to carry out properly the duties delegated to her by Nature of keeping the earth replenished, and has given birth to a bastard son, Jocus, an evil sub-divinity of sexual perversion (prosa v). Switching from mythopœic to conceptual analysis, Nature then ascribes sexual excess ("luxuria") to excess of idleness, food and drink; thus moderation in all things is the best answer to the assaults of sin—vice lies in the extremes.

Nature's analysis of the specific sexual problem is now completed, but her mention of the whole army of sins that attack mankind stimulates her to a poetic outburst (metrum VI) on the ravages of sin in general. Her indignation is too strong for her to analyse the vices in an orderly manner at this point; the turgid rhetoric and confused emotions recall the psychological mood of the first metrum and the *Descriptio Cupidinis*. But once again powerful emotions are brought under control through the application of cool analysis. In the following prosa, in accordance with the dreamer's emphatic request for a more ordered statement,[21] Nature relates at length the characteristics of such natural vices as Gluttony, Avarice, Pride, Jealousy, Flattery and Prodigality, appropriate to the general area of experience in which sexual excess is likely to occur. The account of these negative qualities is balanced and relieved by descriptions of the counterbalancing virtues of Wisdom, Moderation, Chastity, Temperance, Generosity, and Humility. While Alan labours, as poet, to make the virtues more attractive than the vices, he is too careful a theologian to think, with Prudentius, that they can conquer by their own innate strength or attractiveness: Nature in view of the inability of the virtues to stand up to the vices, has to send for her priest, Genius, to excommunicate all those who practise these wickednesses. Man conquers sins not through his own volition but only with ecclesiastically mediated divine assistance, but for such assistance to be meaningful he must first have rejected them, so far as he can, on the natural level.

The dialectical structure of the *Complaint* thus by no means embodies an attempt to gain new intellectual truth as such, but rather to represent the gradual extension of rational control over emotional disorder. We have seen how this is manifested in the identification, description and ordering of the vices and virtues, the process by which the obscurities of the emotional struggle may be resolved. While this dialectical movement is undoubtedly the most important means of representing the re-assertion of self-control, the same principle is at work in other aspects of the dialogue. One sees it in the forcing of distinctions between apparently related spiritual entities, such as Cupid and Jocus, and between *Largitas* and *Prodigalitas* (prosa ix). One sees this principle also in the continual scrutiny and explication that Alan makes of his methods of expressing his ideas. A notable example of this is the apparent interruption of the line of thought in prosa iv, when the dreamer

[21] "Ad haec ego: 'Quoniam in area generalitatis hujus intellectus excursor oberrat, intelligentiae vero specialitas amicatur, vellem ut vitia quae in quodam generalitatis implicas glomicello, speciosissimarum specierum intersticiis discoloribus explicares.'" (*I replied, "Since in the area of these generalities the intellect wanders astray, but the specific is beloved by the intelligence, I should like you to unravel the vices that you wound up into the tangled ball of generality, defining them with contrasting distinctions most discriminatingly in their categories."*)

breaks in to ask if the gods themselves do not transgress against the order of nature, to which Nature replies, in traditional fashion, that the ancient pagan poets either falsified or allegorized. This interchange, which one critic has seen as digressive,[22] appears, however, not only to reflect Boethius's rejection of the pagan muses in the *Consolation* but also to justify Alan's subsequently extensive use of figures of pagan gods in a Christian moral allegory.

One also notices his careful and subtle description of the mode by which Nature speaks to the dreamer:

Quae postquam me mihi redditum intellexit, mentali intellectui materialis vocis mihi depinxit imaginem, et quasi archetypa verba idealiter praeconcepta, vocaliter produxit in actum.

. . . *she drew for my mental understanding the image of a material voice, as she brought into actuality archetypal words, preconceived in the realm of ideas.*

Similarly, Nature refers explicitly to the principle we have already discerned, that confusion or unnaturalness in subject is echoed by deformity in the style of expression:

"Sed tamen aliquando, ut superius libavimus, quia rebus de quibus loquimur cognatos oportet esse sermones, rerum informitati locutionis debet deformitas conformari." (II, p. 468)

developing appropriately a rhetorical principle he must have noted in the *Consolation* (III, end of prosa xii). The dreamer demonstrates the relationship of the verse and prose sections of the *Complaint* when he calls upon Nature to analyse an emotional and poetic general statement into its different aspects and elements, and elsewhere calls upon her to supplement her prose description of *Avaritia* with a fiercer attack in verse: "Vellem ut laxatis reprehensionum habenis, praecordialius Avaritiae filias impugnares." (II, p. 491.) (*I wish you to let slip the reins of reprimand, and assault the daughters of Avarice more vehemently.*)

The dreamer gains mastery over the emotional impulses stirred up in him by the *Venus scelesta* and associated destructive impulses, whether we understand such impulses to take the form of extreme repulsion or attraction towards their manifestations. The *Complaint*

[22] Raynaud De Lage, p. 47.

66

of Nature, slow moving and redundant though it must seem if interpreted as a simple statement of the undesirability of unnatural behaviour, becomes a coherent, purposive and effective work if understood as offering to the reader a process of emotional and psychic integration in which obsessions may be purged both through contemplation of beneficial images and archetypes and through concurrent participation in a dialogue where the areas of disturbance are related in an orderly manner to the universal scheme of things.

IS SEX NECESSARY?

The curiously erotic aura surrounding Nature's role as nurse and mother raised by implication the question of the proper and natural use of the sexual appetites, a question that we may conclude remained on the dreamer's mind, since he later breaks in apologetically upon Nature's discourse in the fourth prosa to demand a description of Cupid. Nature agrees to supply one, adding some rather arch hints about the dreamer himself being anxious to enrol in Cupid's train. The well known "Descriptio Cupidinis" (metrum v) which embodies her reply returns us to the "world upsidedown" topos of the first metrum with its use of oxymoron and antithesis and to the disjointed universe depicted there. But there is a difference. Where the depiction of sexual behaviour in the first metrum emphasized the perversion or reversal of the normal, here the emphasis is on the seemingly inextricable confusion of the good and evil qualities of love: "Pax odio, fraudique fides, spes juncta timori, . . ." (II, p. 472) (*Peace joined to hatred, faith to fraud, hope to fear,* . . .). Nonetheless, the evil seems to outweigh the good in the description, and we are hardly surprised by Nature's concluding advice to flee the times and occasions when Venus can afflict you, for only in flight can she be overcome.

It appears that Alan has brought off the difficult feat of making a case for the celibate life based on natural principles alone. But certain problems remain. It is not explained how the eschewing of Cupid's wars is going to be compatible with Nature's duties, as described in prosa iv (II, p. 470), to keep the earth replenished. There is also some inconsistency in making Venus at once Nature's *subvicaria*, and an enemy to be avoided at all costs. It is quite evident that Alan's answer here is rather an extreme one, valid only for celibate clerics and religious. Not surprisingly, he attempts some solution of these obvious difficulties. At the beginning of the following (fifth) prosa, Nature modifies her position somewhat:

Nec mirandum, si in praetaxata Cupidinis depictione notulas reprehensionis intersero, quamvis ipse mihi quadam consanguinitatis germanae fibula connectatur. . . . Non enim originalem Cupidinis naturam in honestate redarguo, si circumscribatur frenis modestiae, si habenis temperantiae castigetur, . . . sed si ejus scintilla in flammam evaserit, vel ipsius fonticulus in torrentem excreverit, . . . exuberationis tumor solatium medicamenti desiderat; quoniam omnis excessus temperatae mediocritatis incessum disturbat, et abundantiae morbidantis inflatio quasi in quaedam apostemata vitiorum exuberat. (II, p. 474)

It is not strange if in this portrayal of Cupid I intersperse slight signs of blame, although he is allied to me by the connection of own blood relationship. . . . I do not deny that the essential nature of love is honorable if it is checked by the bridle of moderation, if it is restrained by the reins of sobriety. . . . But if its spark shoots into a flame, or its little spring rises to a torrent, . . . the swelling and excess disturbs the progress of well-regulated temperance, and the pride of unhealthy extravagance fattens, so to speak, into impostumes of vices.

Here love is all right in moderation, a good servant but a bad master; what a sensible point of view it seems, and yet hardly a true resolution, since it remains incompatible with Nature's earlier advice to flee from Venus. It is evident that Alan has rather suggested the need for a synthesis than found one. In a sense the whole passage remains episodic and unintegrated, not because of any lack of coherence in thought or skill in construction but because Alan did not understand, and it is not easy to see how he could have understood, where to put passionate love in the scheme of virtues and vices, where to draw the line. Truth is one, but here is something which escapes our categories, on which no final answer seems possible. The ingenuity and rhetorical force of Alan's arguments, combined as they were with obvious weaknesses, came to stimulate a number of modifications and answers by later allegorists, particularly Jean de Meun and Chaucer. Indeed, no poet seriously concerned with questions of earthly love in the general scheme of things could afford to ignore it.

5

The Landscapes of Vision

FROM its earliest traceable beginnings, the dialogue manifested a tendency to break into allegory. In the classical period, the example of Plato's "myths": the vision of the man of Er which closes the *Republic*, the allegory of the charioteers in the *Phaedrus*, and others, stimulated imitations such as Cicero's "Somnium Scipionis" at the end of his *Republic* and parodies such as the ascent to the Olympian heaven in Lucian's comic dialogue, the *Icaromenippus*. Macrobius evidently considered the "Somnium" more important than the dialogue to which it was attached. In the *Consolation of Philosophy* we have seen that life itself, under the pressure of its imminent termination, fuses into allegorical vision. We cannot attribute the tendency towards allegory merely to a wish to imitate Plato; one would rather say that the ancient poet-philosophers sought to transcend the too pure rationality of their formal discourse. The classical writers of dialogue had kept their myths distinct from their conversations; after the *Consolation* the writer of dialogue had an example of the fusion of the two. As we have seen, the most obvious possibility of allegorization in the dialogue lay in the person of the Master or Mistress of Discourse, the merging of whose role with the *potentia* seems to have revived an ancient form of visionary experience.

In this chapter we shall investigate in greater depth the second main type of visionary *imago* through which the classical dialogue became allegorized, the *locus animae* or sacred place, as it manifests itself in the allegorical visions of the Middle Ages. We shall first attempt to elucidate its archetypal dimension, in order to comprehend something of the great imaginative force of the *locus* in the period, as evidenced by the extraordinary frequency of its manifestations in art and literature. Secondly, we shall examine the how rather than the why of the *imago*, and trace the sources and routes by which its various forms entered medieval poetry.

THE SACRED PLACES

C. S. Lewis wrote of the Park of Lord Mirth in Guillaume de Lorris' *Romance of the Rose:*

But, of course, its classical and erotic models only partially account for it. Deeper than these lies the world-wide dream of the happy garden— the island of the Hesperides, the earthly paradise, Tirnanogue. The machinery of allegory may always, if we please, be regarded as a system of conduit pipes which thus tap the deep, unfailing sources of poetry in the mind of the folk and convey their refreshment to lips which could not otherwise have found it.[1]

This comment gives excellent testimony to the effect that certain descriptions in literature and art (as well as experiences in real life) have on us: the evocation of a feeling that through the specific description shines some great human desire or fear that can never be fully understood or elucidated, except through some illumination transcending the normal limits of human experience. Specifically, one is struck by the non-rational character of the emotion. Desire for fame, riches or power seems weak and superficial when measured against the intensity of the desire to attain such a place of archetypal attraction as the paradise garden. Is it possible to throw any light on the secret of its attraction? Let us first consider the nature of the sacred place in general.

Looking as far back into prehistory as our present understanding permits, we can see an era in which gods were associated with and perhaps scarcely distinguishable from "sacred places". Such places might consist of a prominent tree, grove, rock, crag, cave or mountain; in fact any place which could be easily and prominently distinguished from the monotony of the terrain where the tribe had its habitation.[2] At a very early stage there seems to have developed an unconscious analogy between the disturbance of the monotony of the landscape by some prominent feature and the disturbance of the ordinary unreflecting consciousness by some significant idea or concept. Indeed, all abstract ideas seem to have

[1] *Allegory of Love* (Oxford, 1936), pp. 119–20. *Cf.* J. A. W. Bennett, *The Parlement of Foules* (Oxford, 1957), p. 63.
[2] *Cf.* Mircea Eliade, *The Sacred and the Profane* (New York, 1961), chapter 1.

started life as "gods" or "daimons".[3] Ever since, though with
progressively diminishing force, specific abstract ideas have been
identified with specific places, by natural analogy. Today we can
only obtain an idea of the strength of identification of place and
concept by considering the powerful emotional and conceptual
associations of special places we can remember from our childhood,
before instinct was overlaid by the dissociating intellect. For long
periods, moreover, man's nascent rationality was employed in
strengthening rather than opposing such instinctive associations
of concept and place. We find the gods and goddesses first located
in sacred groves (Lat. *templum*), and then in the course of time
usually "civilized" into inhabiting sacred houses (also *templum*) in
the cities.[4] Men visited special locales, grove or temple, to establish
contact with those important concepts and emotions that impinged
upon their lives but were not yet subject to the complete control of
the conscious mind.

In many cases, as we have seen, the most effective contact with
the deity was established during sleep, when the mind would be
especially open to direct intuitions unmediated by the reason.
"Incubation" as a means of obtaining the message of the god was
practised in earliest Sumerian times and as late as the medieval
period. E. R. Dodds has commented on the cultural persistence of
dream imagery:

. . . in many primitive societies there are types of dream structure
which depend on a socially transmitted pattern of belief, and cease to
occur when that belief ceases to be entertained. Not only the choice of
this or that symbol, but the nature of the dream itself, seems to conform
to a rigid, traditional pattern. It is evident that such dreams are closely
related to myth, of which it has been well said that it is the dream-
thinking of the people, as the dream is the myth of the individual.[5]

Around the beginning of the Christian era, communications
from the gods started to come not only in the temples or sacred

---

[3] See Hermann Usener's *Götternamen* (Bonn, 1896), pp. 78, 364–75.
[4] See J. A. MacCulloch's article "Temples" in Hastings's *Encyclopedia
of Religion and Ethics* XII, pp. 236–7.
[5] *The Greeks and the Irrational* (Berkeley, 1963), pp. 103–4. Field
evidence set forth by Dorothy Eggan, "The Personal Use of Myth in
Dreams", in *Myth: A Symposium* edited by Thomas Sebeok (Indiana,
1958), pp. 70–71.

groves, but in independent dreams and visions which, however, still often reproduced the traditional surroundings of the deity, temple, grove or sacred hill. In other words, both the natural and the cultured symbolism surrounding the appearance of the deity became transferred to the dream world and no longer attached to the actual surroundings in which the dreamer might seek the assistance of the god. As was proclaimed by a certain Theodotus, a second-century Montanist prophet:

Pure places and meadows have received voices and visions of holy phantasms. But every man who has been perfectly purified shall be thought worthy of divine teaching and of power.[6]

In the succeeding chapters of this work we shall see numerous instances of the repetition of the cultural patterns of classical Greece and Rome persisting with extraordinary fidelity and intensity right up to the Renaissance. The transfer of the vision to a purely psychic locale was accompanied by development of the brilliant techniques of allegorical and dialectical analysis that the medieval visionary employed to wrest from the visions their secrets of psychic integration. The purposes of the visions were rarely practical—political, medical, or cultic—like those of the ancient world; medieval visionary achievements tended to the spiritual and psychological.

THE PSYCHOLOGY OF LANDSCAPE: WILDERNESS AND CITY

We have noted that the dwelling of the gods, of the *potentiae*, may be found either far away from human habitations in the wilderness, or comfortably domesticated in the cities of men. Landscape symbolism of the Middle Ages or any other period is not easy to

[6] *Ante-Nicene Fathers* (Buffalo, 1886) VIII, p. 47, excerpt 34. E. R. Curtius, in *European Literature and the Latin Middle Ages* (New York, 1953), pp. 198*ff*., gives valuable indications of the manner in which the sacred Vale of Tempe became an inspiration for literary descriptions of the *locus amoenus*. See also Gwyn Williams' study of the similar use that was made of sacred vales in North Africa ("Classic Cyrenaica: An Earthly Paradise", *The Listener*, 17 October, 1957, pp. 603*ff*.)

comprehend without some understanding of the basic psychic polarity of city and wilderness which naturally arises out of man's experience of his environment. It is this polarity, moreover, that can provide us with an important clue to the nature of the attractive power of the *locus amoenus*.

In those early epics which are concerned with the general relations of the hero to his society we see that the poet's starting point is frequently the city, the community. The *Aeneid*, according to Fustel de Coulanges, is in one aspect the greatest work in the genre of poems concerning the founding of cities.[7] The starting point of *Beowulf* is not the *enfances* of the hero but the founding of Danish society by Scyld and its most glorious and concrete manifestation in the building of the hall, *Heorot*. *Gilgamesh* opens with an account of the city, Uruk: "Did not the seven sages lay its foundations?" We see reflected here the fact that the founding of a city is primarily the work of the active rational consciousness. The society the city makes possible is the essential of any ordered conscious life, a repository for traditional wisdom and a frame of reference for thought and speculation. Within it, the festivals of the gods provide ordered outlets for subconscious impulses that might otherwise overwhelm consciousness. But outside lie forest and ocean, not merely symbols of the vast powers of the unconscious, but in early periods at least, the very place of their operation.

In ancient literature, the primary danger to the consciousness inherent in the wilderness is manifested and symbolized in its animal inhabitants. Since man has only uncertainly discerned their shapes and characteristics, and has not yet reduced them to genera and species, their appearances are entirely unpredictable and can hardly be distinguished from the internal menaces of the nightmare. At the frontiers of the unknown, the sleep of reason engenders monsters, apotropaic sentinels warning man away from the psychic disintegration threatened where urban rationality will no longer find its necessary phenomenal correlatives. While the monster embodies the terror engendered by the hostility of featureless terrain to the rational process, the enchantress—the second major peril of the wilderness—incarnates its feminine seductiveness, the temptation for man to yield to anti-rational self-indulgences of the body and spirit, unbridled sexuality or slothful

[7] *The Ancient City* (New York, 1956), pp. 143*ff*. *Cf.* Werner Jaeger, *Paideia* (New York, 1965) I, p. 115.

day-dreaming, away from the restraints of his community and its institutions.

Man is distinct from other animals in that he has continually extended the physical and psychic boundaries of his environment in not only a quantitative but a qualitative sense. These victories, the evidence seems to indicate, have been achieved not by the people as a whole but by inspired individuals whose actions may at first engender considerable misgiving and opposition. In terms of our present analysis, the hero of ancient literature emerges as the man who is able to internalize the psychic achievements of his community and to function in the wilderness as a rational being.

Heroic literature of all periods has thus been frequently concerned with the recording of the victories by which the frontiers of the rational intellect have been extended. The relatively primitive Beowulf epic first celebrates the heroic efforts by which the nascent community of Heorot was freed from the troublous assaults of the monster by night (the time when the powers of the wilderness are at their strongest) and continues by relating the subsequent invasion of the wilderness by day, and the destruction of a monster lurking in the murky depths of the desolate tarn, a place which one can even today sense as threatening to rational equilibrium. In the psychologically more advanced and stable society portrayed in the *Gilgamesh* epic, the monstrous boar Humbaba does not directly attack the mighty city of Uruk, though he represents a menace that the old and wise of the city believe to be too strong to be challenged. The hero and his comrade Enkidu have to make a long journey to the cedar forest where the monster abides, but he remains as much a psychic as a physical threat, as is implied by Enkidu's words to Gilgamesh:

> To safeguard the cedars,
> As a terror to mortals has Enlil appointed him;
> Weakness lays hold on him who goes down to the forest.[8]

Finally the hero masters the monster by meeting and enduring the gaze of his terrible eyes as much as by physical assault.

Thus the hero typically overcomes the monsters, cuts down the forests, and resists the temptations of the unconscious in its attrac-

[8] Translation by E. A. Speiser in *Religions of the Ancient Near East* edited by Isaac Mendelsohn (New York, 1955), p. 65.

tive aspects, as embodied in the enchantresses, the syrens and mermaids, the woodnymphs and *skogsrå*, or, in more sophisticated literature, a Calypso or a Circe.[9] As the result of his victories, the fundamental distinction of human landscape into city and wilderness, known and unknown, undergoes a profound modification: the polarity, once identical in both internal and external consciousness, begins to separate into a physical and a psychic dimension, as it becomes possible for man to bear into the wilderness a city within himself.

It remains to be noted that the fundamental conflict of man and wilderness, perhaps underestimated in modern historical thought, did not escape the ancient philosophers and was inherited by the medieval allegorist in abstract form as well as in poetic imagery. Plato's analysis in the *Timaeus* of the universe as created by the interaction of *nous* and *ananke* (Reason and Necessity or Mind and Matter) was developed by Aristotle into the more familiar conjunction of *nous* and *hyle*, where *hyle* denotes the chaos antecedent to the operation of Form, but literally means "forest".[10] That *hyle* kept, or at least regained, some imagistic force is shown by the fourth century Vergilian commentator Servius's gloss on *Aeneid* I. 314: "quam Graeci *hylen* . . . vocant, poetae nominant silvam, id est, elementorum congeriem, unde cuncta procreantur." (*What the Greeks call* hyle *the poets term* silva, *that is the chaotic mass of elements out of which all things are created*.) We have noted that the *silva* is not only a physical but a psychical entity for the primitive and the sense of this is carried over into the Middle Ages, not only instinctively, but also explicitly as in the commentator's gloss. Servius, in reference to the *silva* in which the Golden Bough is concealed (*Aeneid* VI.131), informs us that by "silvas, tenebras, et

[9] The enchantress of the forest as she appears in European folklore and medieval legend has been studied by Richard Bernheimer in *Wild Men in the Middle Ages* (Harvard, 1952), pp. 33–9, 42–3. The typical progression of the hero's tasks from slaying the monster to resisting temptations of the enchantress will be treated in a forthcoming work by the present writer.

[10] For discussion of the concept of *hyle* from Plato to Chalcidius, see J. C. M. van Winden's *Calcidius on Matter: His Doctrine and Sources* (Leiden, 1959), especially pp. 31*ff*., 145, a lucid study to which I am much indebted. Dr. van Winden, however, does not make use of Servius in his study, nor does he mention the possible influence of Gnostic thinkers, who regarded the *hyle* as totally evil, and termed unenlightened, earthbound men *hylici*.

lustra" (*forests, darksome places and wildernesses*) Vergil signifies "in quibus feritas et libido dominantur" (*those things where wild animal nature and the passions dominate.*)[11] This double interpretation of *silva* as original chaos and as the abode of the darker instincts received more philosophical treatment in the commentary of Chalcidius on Plato's *Timaeus*, a work highly influential on twelfth-century philosophical allegory. Chalcidius devotes a great deal of thought to Plato's concept of Necessity, which he firmly translates as *silva* in language which may well have given later allegorists, such as Alan of Lille, the impression that the use of the equivalent Greek term, *hyle*, has the authority of Plato himself.[12] After proper philosophic deliberation and consideration of the positions of the best authorities, Chalcidius (a Platonist, but almost certainly an orthodox Christian) nonetheless comes to the somewhat unorthodox conclusion that the *silva* is "patibilis animae partis, in qua est aliquid corpulentum mortaleque et corporis simile, autrix est et patrona, . . ." (*the author and protectress of the passive part of the soul, in which there is something corporeal and mortal and similar to a body*). Thus, though God's operations on matter have left it good to a high degree, it still retains traces of its old "naturale vitium" (chapter 297).

The influence of the types of interpretation made by Servius and Chalcidius can be seen very clearly in the work of the twelfth-century allegorist and exegete Bernardus Silvestris, who himself gained his soubriquet through his striking employment of the term *silva* for matter. In his Commentary on the *Aeneid* (VI.179) he

[11] *Lustrum* is inadequately translated by "wilderness" here, for the term in fact does much of Servius's work for him in this passage; its normal meanings include bog, lair of beast, wilderness, brothel, and debauchery, almost the whole range of ideas that he wishes to include in *silva*.

[12] See Alan's *Distinctiones dictionum theologicalium*, art. *Silva*, *Patrologia Latina*, volume 210, column 943, "Dicitur primordialis materia, quae apud Graecos dicitur *yle*, Latine *silva*, quam etiam Plato silvam vocat; quia, sicut silva materiam praebet aedificiis, sic primordialis materia corporibus universis." (In fact, *silva* does not seem to have been used in Latin in the sense of "timber", *pace* Ben Jonson.) Alan may have been misled by the phrasing "Necessitatem porro nunc appellat *hylen*, . . ." in Chalcidius, *Platonis Timaeus interprete Chalcidio cum eiusdem commentario*, chapter 268, into reversing the syntactic order of the two objects of *appellat*. In chapter 308 Chalcidius expressly denies that Plato employed the term *hylen* itself for matter. Quotations from Chalcidius are from J. H. Waszink's edition in the *Corpus Platonicum Medii Aevi* (London, 1962).

interprets *in silvam* as "in collectionem temporalium bonorum, umbrosam et inviam quia non est nisi umbra" (*into the assemblage of the good things of this world, shady and pathless because it consists of nothing but shadows*). The Trojans who cut down the trees in this wood are interpreted as "philosophantes" uprooting the temporal vices from the soul.[13] The interpretation may be overspecific and overintellectualized by modern critical standards, but seems in essential harmony with the spirit of the action depicted.

Bernardus's greater work, the *De Mundi Universitate* gives full epic and allegorical expression to the process sketched out in Chalcidius's commentary, by which the original *silva* achieved rebirth into the highest degree of goodness possible to one suffering from "praeponderante malitia" (I, 11), an ultimately incorrigible resistance to the shaping power of *Nous*. The *De Mundi* first shows the *silva* shaped by the species, then in a magnificent, sometimes soaring, sometimes fanciful, poetic catalogue describes the creation of the heavenly bodies, mountains, beasts, rivers, trees, fruits, spices, flowers, etc. The second book is reserved for the creation of man. The work is one of the purest examples of the process in which medievals took such great pleasure—that by which chaos is resolved by the ordering and naming of things.[14]

We shall see later in our discussion of the *Divine Comedy* how Dante combined the intertwined philosophical and psychological aspects of the dark forest in a single image, and fused them together in a manner which recaptures not only the intellectual but the emotional and intuitional force of the primary image.[15]

One typical landscape remains to be accounted for—the enclosed garden, park or paradise, the *locus amoenus*, portrayed as intensely desirable, and situated either very remotely or behind inhibiting physical or psychic barriers. In medieval literature and art these are in origin closely connected with the sacred groves of

[13] *Commentum Bernardi Silvestris* super sex libros Eneidos Virgilii, nunc primum edidit Guilielmus Riedel (Gryphiswaldae, 1924).

[14] *De Mundi Universitate* libri duo, edited by Wrobel & Barach (Innsbruck, 1876).

[15] William Nelson, in *The Poetry of Edmund Spenser* (New York, 1963), pp. 158–62, traces the influence of Servius's interpretation of Vergil's *silva* on Renaissance commentators and poets, who maintained the double interpretation, cosmological and moral, developed in the Middle Ages from Servius and Chalcidius. I should acknowledge here the personal debt I owe to Professor Nelson for pointing out the importance of Servius's interpretations of the *silva* to the understanding of medieval allegorical landscape.

the pagan gods, manifested in an internalized form. In terms of our present analysis they also represent a reconciliation of wilderness and city, the hostile powers of nature tamed but not extinguished, or, psychologically, reason and intuition harmonized, a Blakean marriage of Heaven and Hell. Thus in literature the paradisal garden is often the scene of (or even represents) the solution of a problem.[16]

But the garden has another aspect—the wilderness of the sub-conscious or pre-conscious mind viewed as desirable. These are the deceptive gardens of enchantresses, of worldly, sensual ways of thought or feeling—Circe's Aiaia, the Park of Mirth in the *Romance of the Rose*, Bosch's or Cranach's Garden of Earthly Delights, or Ariosto's Isle of Alcina. The two gardens reflect the contrasting types of spiritual transcendence analysed by Aldous Huxley in an appendix to his work, *The Devils of Loudun*. Huxley contrasts the mystical "deep-seated urge to self-transcendence", "the hard, ascending way" against the "search for bogus liberation, either below or to one side of [one's] personality" in which "the quality of consciousness" is changed by such crude agents as "elementary sexuality", alcohol, drugs or crowd delirium.

THE SOURCES OF ALLEGORICAL LANDSCAPE

This account of allegorical landscape in medieval visions would not be complete without a brief survey of the range of specific literary sources which the allegorist could draw upon, to establish that dimension of the landscape we have called imagistic. The striking variety of sources drawn upon by allegorists as well as the frequency of the appearance of the motif of the sacred place, the *locus animae*, suggest the great attractive power of the archetype in this period.

The primary source of the *imago* was the Biblical Garden of Eden and the garden imagery of the *Song of Songs*. Owing to their general currency, they provided a reference easily comprehensible to the allegorist's audience and were thus susceptible to subtle modification for satirical and parodistic purposes.[17] The archetypal

[16] See below, pp. 92, 95, 98, 129ff, 146ff.
[17] See below, pp. 98, 101, 104.

and psychological nature of such gardens by no means escaped exegetical comment; Augustine recognized not only a physical paradise as the place where man was first created but a spiritual paradise as every place where the soul is in a state of well-being or grace.[18]

It has been suggested that Patristic and medieval Biblical exegesis provides a sure key to the interpretation of the appearance of the *locus amoenus* in any medieval literary text. D. W. Robertson's paper "The Doctrine of Charity in Medieval Literary Gardens" makes the important point that underlying the contemporary interpretation of such gardens would be an awareness of the contrasted gardens of charity and cupidity that frequently appear in the scriptural commentary of the period.[19] Robertson's investigations of the exegetical tradition, though undeniably a major contribution to medieval scholarship, involve the assumption that writers of secular poetry wished to express precisely the same point of view as the theologians, that secular literature was no more than ecclesiastical literature in disguise. In fact, if this method of interpretation were to be found plausible, it would hardly be necessary to interpret any medieval garden in any other terms than those of Charity and Cupidity. With this master key to open all doors, any general discussion of the differing traditions of medieval literary landscapes such as we attempt here would be useless and misleading.

One could conceive of the existence of such a literature and might agree that medieval literature is of this type if sufficient corroborative proof were adduced. But the plausibility of the hypothesis is slight. It seems difficult to interpret the *Beowulf* poet, Chrétien, Andreas Capellanus, Guillaume de Lorris and Jean de Meun, and Chaucer in "The Merchant's Tale", as employing the symbolism of the garden in precisely the same way as Hugh of St. Victor or Rabanus Maurus. On other grounds one would judge the more secular minded writers and poets as somewhat ambiguous in their attitude towards the strictly Christian life, and it seems easier to believe that this ambiguity is echoed in their garden imagery than to make the garden imagery a clue to an orthodoxy not otherwise manifested.

If one looks at Robertson's interpretations of specific texts, one

[18] *De Genesi ad Litteram* XII.34, and see Howard Patch, *The Other World* (Cambridge, 1950), p. 143.
[19] *Speculum* 26 (January, 1951), pp. 24–49.

finds that in fact it seems very difficult to coax them into supporting his general hypothesis. One may instance his treatment of the enchanted mere in *Beowulf*, which is termed an evil (deceptive) garden. To this one can only answer in the words of the poet "Nis þæt hēoru stōw" (line 1372: which one might render: "It isn't a pleasant place at all.") For an evil garden, as generally understood, and as Robertson elsewhere in the article shows, must present at first appearance a pleasant impression. The mere-dweller Grendel is descended from Cain and the giants of *Genesis*, but this hardly permits us to interpret him "figuratively" as "the type of the militant heretic or worldly man". For in no sense does he act in this way in the poem, but simply as a loathsome fiend, God's enemy. The poet has not left us ill-supplied with definitions and descriptions of his character. Other particulars of the description, the frosty trees, the fire on the water (uninterpreted by Robertson), the monsters that swim in it, and the hart that would give up its life on the shore rather than enter such a lake, are all part of the elementary horror of the description.[20] There may be overtones of Christian ideas of Hell, (or, for that matter, of the Nordic niflheim) but it does not help one's reading of the poem to force such an identification despite the evidence of the text.

Before quitting this aspect of our topic, one should note the possible influence of early Christian visionary allegory in the later Middle Ages. The vision of the ninth similitude of the *Pastor of Hermas* (second century) includes a detailed description and interpretation of the contrasted topographies of twelve mountains, representing twelve contrasted spiritual states. In the *Symposium* of Methodius (late third century?) the garden in which the banquet takes place is reached by an allegorical journey over a rough and arduous path endangered by reptiles and precipices. The symposium itself is held in the garden of *Arete*, a *locus* both *amoenus* and *conclusus*, abounding with flowers and fruits, irrigated by fountains and rivulets, and cooled by soft breezes, a fittingly remote and exalted place for ten maidens to discourse and allegorize on the topic of virginity, the main substance of the work.[21]

These visions contain examples of the two types of allegorical *loci* most prevalent in later medieval allegory: the landscape as

[20] *Beowulf*, 1357–79.
[21] For *Hermas* and the *Symposium* see *The Ante-Nicene Fathers*, II.9 and VI.309, respectively.

setting for the *potentia* or Mistress of Discourse, and the contrast of landscapes to express contrasted psychological and spiritual states. Since both these works were written in Greek and were little known in the western Church, it is not possible to claim that they were the direct sources of the use of allegorical *loci* in the late medieval works that are our chief concern here. But it would probably not be a very hard task to demonstrate a transmission of these commonplace images in visions, allegories and sermons, from the early Christian period to the twelfth century.[22]

Classical sources were combined freely with the Christian even from the earliest times, as the example of Methodius's *Symposium* demonstrates. The most widespread influence seems to have been the Ovidian, particularly in respect of a quite well-defined type of medieval literary topography, the abode of the *potentia*. The models were the dwellings of Famine (*Metamorphosis* VIII.790), the House of Morpheus (XI.950), and the House of Rumour (XII.40). Some medieval treatments of the type are no more than imitative expansions of the Ovidian original: Jean de Meun's land of Hunger (*Roman* 10510ff.), and Chaucer's Cave of Morpheus (*Duchess* 155ff.), and Houses of Fame and Rumour are of this type. But Jean de Hanville's Court of Ambition (*Architrenius* IV), Andreas Capellanus' Palace of Love in the fifth dialogue in the *De Arte Honeste Amandi*, Jean de Meun's abodes of Fortune (*Roman* 6180ff.), and Gawain Douglas's Palace of Honour, among many others, appear to be original creations more or less in Ovidian style, in which the poet attempts something of a *tour de force* by the use of what might be called creative fancy.

Ovid may also have provided the medievals with the model of the *locus* as scene of debate between two contending *potentiae*. The charming prefatory poem to the third book of the *Amores* opens with the poet wandering into an ancient grove, the haunt of woodland deities:

> Stat vetus et multos incaedua silva per annos;
> credibile est illi numen inesse loco.
> fons sacer in medio speluncaque pumice pendens,
> et latere ex omni dulce queruntur aves.

[22] For the vision literature of the period see Howard Patch, *The Other World*, chapter 4; the possibility of oriental influences on medieval visionary painting and poetry is discussed by Hannah Closs in "The Visionary Landscape", *The Aryan Path* (May 1953).

A wood there stands uncut of long years space.
Tis credible some godhead haunts the place.
In midst thereof a cave and sacred spring
Where round about small birds most sweetly spring.
(After Marlowe)

Here he is visited by the spirits of Elegy and Tragedy who fall into debate on their respective attractions in order to persuade the poet to their particular allegiance. This light hearted contention—decided in favour of frivolous Elegy—surely parodies more serious experiences. The use of such words as *numen* and *sacer* suggest, moreover, that the ancient awe of the gods lies closer to the surface in this encounter with the *potentiae* of the wilderness than in the case of the cooler and more detached descriptions of their abodes in the *Metamorphoses*.[23] The incident as a whole functions as one of the forms taken by the topos of rejection, and would appear to be an important literary ancestor of the frequent medieval debates and contentions that take place in the *locus amoenus*.

The classical contributions to the manifestations of the *locus amoenus* are too extensive to be treated here in any detail; there is, however, no lack of such descriptions of these *loci* in scholarly works. E. R. Curtius, for example, traces the "ideal landscape" back to Homer, with whom, it is rather dubiously contended, the "western transfiguration of . . . the earth . . . begins."[24] Curtius interprets the *locus amoenus* as a rhetorical topos deriving from the "argumentum a loco" when applied to the eulogy, and from the *descriptio*. Rhetorical theory, as a series of rules for composition, is normally a distillation of literary experience, so that one is usually in doubt as to whether a poet is following the prescriptions of the

[23] See also Lucian's equally frivolous debate between the Lady of Statue Making and Lady Education, who discuss his future career in his *Somnium*. Prodicus's myth of the "Choice of Heracles" (reported in Xenophon, *Memorabilia* II.1.21) would also seem to be a sophisticated handling of this theme, similarly deriving from direct religio-psychic experience.

[24] Curtius, p. 185. It would seem to be hazardous to assess a starting point for the "western transformation of the earth". Even in the epic tradition, the Sumerian paradise of Dilmun (Mendelsohn, pp. 4ff.) precedes the Island of Syria in the *Odyssey* (XC.403); the Island of Utnapishtim the Faraway (Mendelsohn, pp. 99ff.) anticipates Menelaus's Elysium (*Odyssey* IV.565). Few primitive peoples seem to be without legends of such places, as the article "Abode of the Blest" in Hastings's *Encyclopaedia of Religion and Ethics* succinctly demonstrates.

rhetorician in describing a *locus amoenus*, or making his own distillation from works he has read, or even whether, in the case of a dream vision, he has, as he claims, actually had a visionary experience, expressed in terms of the prevailing cultural imagery.[25] Rhetorical theory tends to account for only the most uninspired, and thus unimportant, developments of the topic.

[25] Literary historians have taken too little account of the possibility that medieval poets were often being strictly truthful when they claimed to be describing an actual visionary experience. Lydgate's lines at the conclusion of the *Assembly of the Gods*, (edited by O. Triggs, The Early English Text Society, 1896, 2043–65) suggest something of the inspiration for the composition of a dream allegory:

> Whyche doon, fro slepe I gan to awake.
> My body all in swet began for to shake
> For drede of the syght that I had seene,
> Wenyng to me all had be trew
>
> Actuelly doon where I had beene,
>   The batayll holde twene Vyce & Vertew.
> But when I sy hit, hit was but a whew,
>   A dreme, a fantasy, & a thyng of nought.
>   To study theron I had nomore thought.
>
> Tyll at the last I gan me bethynke
>   For what cause shewyd was thys vysyon.
> I knew nat; wherfore I toke pen & ynke
>   And paper to make therof mencion
>   In wrytyng, takyng consideracion
>   That no defaute were founde in me,
>   Wheron accusyd I ought for to be
>
> For slowthe, that I had left hit vntolde—
>   Nowthyr by mowthe nor in remembraunce
> Put hit in wrytyng; wher thorow manyfolde
>   Weyes of accusacion myght turne me to greuaunce,
>   All thys I saw as I lay in a traunce,
>   But whedyr hit was with myne ey bodyly
>   Or nat in certayn, God knoweth and nat I.

6

Landscape and Dialogue

BOETHIUS and Alan of Lille had both incorporated philosophic contemplation of the cosmos into a more general process of psychotherapy designed to put man into harmony with the moral and spiritual order of the universe. While the theme of cosmic contemplation continues, if only in vestigial form, in a great number of visionary allegories of the later Middle Ages, these subsequent visions are marked by a re-emergence of the sacred landscapes of the mythopœic era, the mysteries of grove and sanctuary. Visionary poets increasingly employ, furthermore, systematic contrast of these landscapes to express fine distinctions in the quality of experience represented. The *potentia*, now often in the form of a goddess in her sanctuary, continues her philosophic dialogues with the visionary, though with some diminution of rigour and seriousness at times, particularly in the case of vernacular works.

While later medieval allegory is thus characterized by subtle interrelationships of the three main elements of visionary authority, dialogue, and landscape, we cannot claim any particular originality for this association. Socrates's dialogue with Phaedrus in the grove of the Ilissian nymphs[1] and the discourse of Aeneas and Anchises in Vergil's Elysium anticipate, with comparable subtlety, the greatest of the medieval visions in the use of these elements. In the early Christian visions of the *Pastor of Hermas* and the *Symposium* of Methodius we find the medieval type of theological and psychotherapeutic dialogue substantially established.

Visionary allegory in the later Middle Ages still arises out of the hero's anguish, though developments in structure and subject-matter reshape its manifestations. In the great allegorical epics of the twelfth century, the *De Mundi Universitate* of Bernardus Sylvestris and Alan of Lille's *Anticlaudianus*, the psychic crisis, which initiates the metaphysical action of the drama, affects the

[1] *Cf.* Adam Parry, "Landscape in Greek Poetry", *Yale Classical Studies* XV (1957), pp. 3–29.

potentiae rather than any human hero, as in the fervent longing of Bernard's Nature for the rebirth of the *silva* (matter), or in the anguish of Alan's Nature and her attendant powers at the depravity of man and the natural world. While these metaphysical epics, lacking a visionary hero, strictly speaking lie outside our scope, they present an important related psycho-literary pattern. The main action of these epics concerns the efforts of such relatively access-ible *potentiae* as Nature or Prudence to ameliorate the condition of the natural world through the interposition of higher, celestial, *potentiae* such as Nous and Urania. When man finally appears he is presented from the outside as created and guided by the *potentiae*. These allegories thus depict man as seen through the eyes of the *potentiae*, a strange reversal of viewpoint, which provides an indica-tion of the astonishing degree of imaginative reality these figures had acquired in this period, and some measure of the gulf which separates twelfth-century consciousness from our own.

There also arises a tendency, with the development of a greater range of topics treated in visionary dialogue, towards a greater range in the emotions that spark off the initial psychic crisis. In particular, allegory becomes an unexpectedly effective form to express the emotions and deliberations of a love affair—almost every element proves to be adaptable from moral to erotic psycho-therapy. But while concern with the salvation of the soul naturally proceeds from serious and sometimes profound states of feeling, the concern of the erotic dreamer varies in intensity from the polished insouciance of the amorous courtiers in Andreas Capellanus's *Art of Courtly Love* to the anguished melancholia of Francesco Colonna in the *Hypnerotomachia*. The erotic vision consequently manifests two conflicting tendencies, often both present in the same work, firstly to treat limited utilitarian questions of a less momentous character than those of the philosophical visions of the past, and secondly to explicate the problems of earthly love in the light of the divine agape, from which the reality of the erotic ultimately derives, in order to reconcile the two loves in a single synthesis.

THE "ARCHITRENIUS"

Many of these new tendencies can be found in seminal form within Alan's *Complaint of Nature*. We have already seen how Alan raised questions concerning the nature of Eros which were to be taken up more extensively in later allegory. So far as use of landscape is concerned, he had already achieved something of the effect of a *locus amoenus* for his Lady Nature in the elaborate description of the rejoicing of the natural world at her arrival. Not surprisingly, too, in such a work bristling with dialectical and rhetorical antitheses, landscape itself comes to be used antithetically in the topos of rejection implied in the contrast of Cupid and Jocus:[2]

Ille albis inargentatos nitoribus argenteos fontes inhabitat; iste loca perenni aridate damnata indefesse concelebrat. Iste in deserta planitie figit tentoria; illi vallis complacet nemorosa. (II, p. 481)

The former dwells by silvery fountains gleaming in argent splendour; the latter does not tire of frequenting places condemned to perpetual aridity. He pitches his camp in a desert plain while woody haunts in the valleys please the former.

The Complaint of Nature was shortly followed by a verse allegory in nine books, the *Architrenius*, by a poet variously known as Johannis de Altavilla, Jean de Hautville, or Hanville. Although probably unknown to Chaucer, it had a considerable influence on later allegories such as the *Roman de la Rose* and makes a wider use of landscape for allegorical purposes than any previous work. The *Architrenius* has not received much sustained scholarly attention. The only recent text, edited by Thomas Wright *c.* 1872,[3] often

---

[2] Alan was not the first poet to juxtapose landscapes in this way. Such literary contrasts reflect the fundamental antithesis between heaven and hell. His most influential literary predecessor was Vergil, who in the sixth book of the *Aeneid* tidied up the ideas of the underworld and life after death he had found in the work of earlier poets and philosophers. We find there a kind of poetic analysis of the fates of man after death, first by type of man, warrior, lover, etc., and then by moral virtue, in accordance with which criterion the soul is sent either to punishment in the castle of Rhadamanthus or to reward and happiness in the Elysian fields. In the Ninth Similitude of the *Hermas* twelve mountains with contrasting terrains, favourable or unfavourable, represent twelve constrasted spiritual states. Nearer Alan's particular usage we find in Prudentius' *Harmartigenia* (789–801) two brothers described as having to choose between a good and a wretched life in terms of paths through *amoena virecta*, or through *spinea silva* and along a *margine clivoso*. But the former leads to *caenosas paludes*, the latter to *sideribus propinquis*. (*cf.* Prodicus's "Choice of Heracles" in Xenophon's *Memorabilia* II.1.21–34).

[3] The text of the *Architrenius* is in *The Anglo Latin Poets of the Twelfth Century* I. (London, 1872). Concerning commentaries, see Pierre Louis

appears incoherent, and, though the work was the subject of commentaries in the succeeding centuries, there appear to have been no translations. Jean possessed a stimulating unconventionality of mind which, combined with his complicated syntax and delight in neologisms, makes him slow reading for those of average Latinity.

The psychotherapeutic scheme of the *Architrenius* is not dissimilar to that of the *Complaint*. After hearing something of the poet's own struggles with *accedia* and other vices, we learn that Architrenius, the "arch-weeper", is (like the poet) a young man who, scrutinizing his soul, finds nothing virtuous there, and comes to the conclusion that Nature should have protected him better against the assaults of vice.

> mersosque profunda
> Explorat sub mente lares, nec moribus usquam
> Invenit esse locum, nec se virtutibus unum
> Impendisse diem; "Mene istos," inquit, "in usus
> Enixa est Natura parens? me misit ut arma
> In superos damnata feram, . . .?
> . . . mater quid pignora tantae
> Destituit labi, nec quem produxit alumno
> Excubat, ut nullis maculam scelus inspuet actis?"
> (I, pp. 247–8)

He explores the hidden abodes within the recesses of his mind and he finds no place there consecrated to morality, nor can he discover that he has ever remained virtuous for as long as a single day. "Did Nature, my mother really bring me into the world for practices such as these?" he wonders. "Did she send me out to take up arms against the gods, like a lost soul? . . . Should a mother abandon her offspring to such a fate, instead of watching the child she has brought up to ensure that his actions do not become tainted by sin?"

Since Nature is all powerful and is able to produce all sorts of monsters,[4] the train of thought appears to continue, she should be

Ginguené, *Histoire Littéraire de la France*, XIV (Paris, 1869) p. 570, and Kuno Franke, "Der Architrenius des Johann von Anville", *Forschungen zur Deutschen Geschichte* XX (1880), pp. 475–6.

4 The first examples in a long catalogue of these monsters are Cornelia and "Aristonie" who were *gemini sexus* and reversed the natural order of things in their marriages. The situation, and the punning language in which it is described, remind us of the first metrum of the *Complaint of*

able to protect Architrenius. He therefore decides to go out and search the world for Nature's answer to his difficulties.

> . . . profugo natura per orbem
> Est quaerenda mihi; veniam quamcunque remotos
> Abscondat secreta lares, odiique latentes
> Eliciam causas, et rupti forsan amoris
> Restituam nodos, . . .   (I, p. 251)

I must go as an exile through the world to seek for Nature; I shall attempt to reach whatever secret place it is she has concealed her far-off abodes, and there search out the hidden causes of sin, and, if it may be, join once again the sundered links of love.

The two passages taken together give us a striking insight into the processes of allegorical creation. In the first passage the "lares" are "mersos . . . profunda . . . sub mente"; in the second they are "remotos" and must be searched for "per orbem". A mere hundred lines separate the passages, so that the transition from seminal image to allegory implies a transformation of the external world into a new realm of the mind which will obey the laws of the inner life before those of the outer, a realm awaiting the explorations of the mental traveller.

The term "lares" is used here with particular felicity. It indicates one's dwelling and at the same time the place where the gods make their most personal contact with the individual, as opposed to their relationship with his tribe or city. The transition from the outer to the inner world could not have been suggested to the reader with such evocativeness and clarity were it not for the extraordinary use the poet makes of this term, which for Jean seems to have the meaning of "shrines" or "abodes" as well as "spirits".[5] For the first time

---

Nature. There seems to be hidden ambiguity here, turning on the attribution to *Natura* of creating what Alan found most unnatural. Architrenius's complaints against *Natura* reach such proportions in the last book that the work might almost have been titled *De Planctu contra Naturam*. In the last book of the *De Arte Honeste Amandi*, Andreas finally abandons his onslaughts on the female character, "lest we be thought in some way to accuse nature. . . ." (*The Art of Courtly Love*, translated by Parry, New York, 1941, p. 198).

[5] We have noted above p. 23 a similar use of the term *penates* in Statius' *Thebaid*. Ducange cites *lar* only as meaning *hearth* or *home* in this period, but Latham's *Revised Mediaeval Latin Word List* quotes a thirteenth-century use of the term *lares ecclesie* in the sense "the bosom of the church".

the seminal image of the allegory refers to a feature of the landscape rather than to a personification; in view of this, we shall not be surprised to find that landscapes play a more important role in Jean's work than in that of earlier allegorists. Nonetheless, there is no sharp break away from the use of personifications as a basis for the seminal image. Each time the term *lares* is used allegorically, it is intimately connected with a personification. Apart from the *lares Naturae*, the abodes of *Ambitio* and *Superbia*, both visited by the hero in the course of his travels, are also called *lares* (I, pp. 293–311). The term thus becomes a means of transforming not only personifications into mental forces, but their shrines into allegorized landscapes, often of some subtlety of depiction. Jean provides us with perhaps the most effective statement we have encountered of the fact that the poet turning to allegory is entering the world of the inner life. Thus Architrenius, distantly descended, one might say, from Gilgamesh and Aeneas, becomes the first of the interior pilgrims, wandering over the world in search of his soul, and—like Dante, Bunyan's Christian, and Kafka's Land-surveyor—*profugus*, an exile, searching out the *lares*, numinous abodes of mental divinities, in a landscape at once internal and external.

Apart from providing us with our first examples of sustained landscape allegory, Jean's text also gives us indications of what one might call the seed-bed of this type of allegory, metaphors that betray the habit of thinking of mental events in terms of place. *Moeroris abyssi, stagna lacrimae, inhospita tecta pudoris*, are examples of the type of metaphor he uses.[6] In the case of the phrase *diis invisa palus* in Architrenius's soliloquy of self-analysis (I, p. 248) we might imagine we are encountering nothing more than a reference to the Styx (Ovid: *Stygiae paludes*), but a helpful glossator of one of the manuscripts explains the phrase as "corpus meum".

Few writers of sustained allegories attempt to express everything they have to say in completely allegorical terms. But the *Architrenius* shows an unusual freedom in this respect. The hero is permitted to move from the "Veneris domus aurea" to student life

---

[6] Like much other of Jean's stylistic rhetorical usages, this use of metaphor was probably inspired by Alan, in whose *Complaint* "Invidia" is termed "erroneae caecitas abyssus, humanae mentis infernus" (Wright, II. 497). In his *Distinctiones* Alan glosses *abyssus* "Dicitur cor hominis profundum et inscrutabile . . . Dicitur cor pravi hominis, unde in Job: Abyssus dixit: non est in me . . ." (Patrologia Latina volume 210, column 689–90).

in Paris, and from there to the sky-grazing Mount of Ambition and the less impressive Hill of Presumption. He then spends a considerable time on the Island of Thule listening to famous philosophers discoursing of vice and virtue, and finally passes to the abode of *Natura*, where all problems are solved by his marriage to *Moderantia*. The general effect is thus that of an autobiography in which various types of experience are expressed in differing modes of presentation, with no particular regard for logical consistency of form. While the *Architrenius* is not explicitly a vision poem, its scheme of representation reflects the visionary, intuitive character of most allegorical representation in this period.

The landscapes display a subtlety and discrimination in presentation worthy of Spenser. The Mount of Ambition is introduced with an appropriate rhodomontade of almost Renaissance dimensions:

> Mons surgente jugo Pellaeam despicit urbem
> Astra supercilio libans, lunaque minorem
> Miratur longe positam decrescere terram
> Sideribus vicinus apex, . . .   (I, p. 292)

> *A Mount there stands whose haughty brows stare down*
> *Where the Macedonian conqueror first saw day.*
> *Its summit scrapes the stars; the lofty peak,*
> *Neighboured among the orbs, admires to see*
> *The far-off Earth shrunk smaller than the Moon.*

On the slopes of the mountain we encounter the "mixed forest" in an unusual development.

> . . . Zephyris ubi succuba tellus
> Veris alumnat opes, passimque intexit amara
> Dulcibus, et fruticum nodis armantur olivae,
> Et laurus cristata rubis, suspectaque dumis
> Quercus, . . .   (I, p. 293)

Here the Earth Mother brings soothing nourishment on the spring breezes for her abundant offspring, and now and then mixes harsh things among the pleasant; the peaceful olives are defended by tangled thickets, and the victorious laurel and the revered oak stand among briers and thorn bushes.

At the top of the mountain is a beautiful garden from which infertile trees are excluded and where the productive are welcomed. But the Court of Ambition, the dwelling of those who attain the top of the mountain, is a place of treachery and frustration, as poets seem usually to find the houses of the great. Moreover, the roots of the mountain, with psychological as well as geological appropriateness, are described as extending as far down into the earth as Tartarus itself.

The Mount of Ambition is, in fact, an allegorical landscape of some complexity. The underlying pattern is a parody of the conception of the earthly paradise. Contemporary thinkers such as Alexander Neckham discussed whether the mountain on which the earthly paradise was conventionally situated penetrated into the sphere of the moon.[7] The mixed forest on the slopes of the mountain is a modification of the grove of the *locus amoenus* to constitute a variation on the traditional barriers against entrance to the earthly paradise. The exclusion of the infertile trees in favour of the fertile is also to be found in the description of the earthly paradise in Alexander Neckham's *De Naturis Rerum* (II.XLIX). The Mount of Ambition is thus a calculated and outrageous blasphemy, in its effect remarkably similar to Tamburlaine's ambitious outburst:

> Our souls, whose faculties can comprehend
> The wondrous architecture of the world,
> And measure every wandering planet's course,
> Still climbing after knowledge infinite,
> And always moving as the restless spheres,
> Will us to wear ourselves, and never rest,
> Until we reach the ripest fruit of all,
> That perfect bliss and sole felicity,
> The sweet fruition of an earthly crown.
> (Marlowe, (I *Tamburlaine* II. VII)

In relation to the poem as a whole, the Mount states in terms of landscape what we have just learned by direct description, that the path of worldly ambition leads to frustration. The students of Paris have to go through every kind of hardship to obtain their degrees, only to find that the "establishment" distrusts the able and learned graduate and prefers the incompetent.

But this argues no distrust of study itself. On Thule we learn

---

[7] See Howard Patch, *The Other World* (Cambridge, 1950), p. 151. Statius's description of Mount Taenarum (*Thebaid* II.32*ff.*) may have been an inspiration, especially since it also was associated with Tartarus.

the true wisdom of the philosophers in respect of Architrenius's original problem of his vulnerability to sin (a problem from which Venus and *Ambitio* at times appear to distract him). The philosophers, anticipating Dante's Limbo, have their own pleasance where they live among undying flowers, free from the assaults of age or climate. The pleasance is under the care of a "loci deitas nativa" whose name is not at this point revealed.

The discourses of the philosophers seem to do no more than accentuate Architrenius's bitterness. Finally, however, Solon tells the story of Polemon, a dissolute young man who went to a lecture by Xenocrates only to scoff, but was instantly converted by the sage to an austere and philosophic life. The way is thus prepared for Architrenius's own conversion, an experience Jean represents, with a brilliant transition, in a different allegorical mode. Architrenius looks up and sees the goddess Nature standing in transcendent splendour on a flowery plain, the *locus amoenus* of the final solution of his problems. Here the Earth Mother no longer, as on the Mount of Ambition, mixes bitter things along with the sweet, but

vere marito
Praegnativa parit rosulas et lilia tellus;   (I. p. 369)

the implication of marriage hinting at the next stage of the poem's development.

For Nature finally turns Architrenius from his weeping by giving him *Moderantia* to wife. *Moderantia* receives the girdle of Venus from Nature as a wedding gift, but attention is not fixed so exclusively on her physical charms as it was in the case of the girl who so attracted Architrenius in the Palace of Venus. Rather, she serves as an answering principle to Ambition, Presumption, Gluttony, Avarice and the other vices we have encountered during the poem. The work concludes with the poet's wishes for the lasting success of their marriage.

The hero's challenge to Nature which opens the main action of the poem, and is repeated in his final confrontation with her, represents a vigorous and refreshing return to the greater intellectual discordances of the Boethian, if not the Platonic, dialogue. Jean Hanville may well have taken seriously the dictum of Boethius's Lady Philosophy: "Sed visne rationes ipsas invicem collidamus? Forsitan ex huiusmodi conflictatione pulchra quaedam veritatis scintilla dissiliat" (*Consolation* III.xii). (*But do you wish our arguments to clash against each other? Perhaps some beautiful spark of truth will shoot out from the collision.*) Indeed, the *Architrenius* stands out even among twelfth-century allegories in the humanistic breadth and boldness of its challenge to contemporary world views, and the search for answers to man's spiritual problems in the natural rather than the supernatural universe. Not only does earthly authority leave the hero unmoved, but Nature herself has considerable difficulty in getting him to accept her solutions to his anxieties. The moralizings of her philosophers on virtue and vice leave him unconsoled. Her cosmological explications of the order and benevolence of God's universe seem admirable to the hero, but he complains that they are too far above his head to assuage his doubts and anxieties, as if implying that the cosmic contemplation which had played such a large part in the spiritual enlightenment of Boethius and Alan was too exalted for him. Architrenius does not protest, however, at Nature's solution of his problem in terms of man's free will. Nature has provided man with all things necessary for a happy, sinless life; his unhappiness is his own responsibility. But apparently much more effective than this rational defence of her position is Nature's description and eulogy of his bride to be, *Moderantia*, the embodiment of the principle on which his psychic healing is to be based; in this respect his bride plays a role analogous to that of Nature herself in the *Complaint*. Nevertheless, the healing of the hero through marriage with *Moderantia* remains as psychologically mysterious in its way as the healing of the dreamer of the *Complaint* through the excommunication pronounced by Genius. In each case it seems more plausible to regard the final act of the vision as proceeding from and symbolic of the total process of self-analysis rather than of independent validity. Moderation seems to be a principle that was lacking not only in every *locus animae* that he visited, but also in the excessive length and emotional intensity of his own reactions to these abuses: marriage with *Moderantia* becomes not merely a synecdoche of the harmony of a life concordant with natural principles, but an assurance of the inner peace that acceptance of the natural universe will bring.

While the hero is finally successful in linking once more the sundered chain of love, he does not achieve this victory in quite the same fashion as Alan: the moral and cosmological consolations characteristic of Alan's work are incorporated but not fully accepted; furthermore, the impulses of natural sexual love, already accepted in a limited and qualified way in the *Complaint*, are here given much greater emphasis as a principle of psychic healing. We might ascribe the latter merely to differences in the personal psychology of the two poets—we have no evidence that Jean was in celibate orders—but it may be noted that in future visionary dialogues this tendency to see in human love the main principle for the healing of psychic disorder is sustained and developed.

PARODIES OF LOVE

The fifth dialogue of Andreas's *Art of Love* exemplifies the effortless manner in which the twelfth-century writer of an erotic treatise might adapt the conventions of visionary allegory to his own purposes. Andreas's dialogue not only parodies a vision of heavenly love, but also incorporates the specific means by which such visions are expressed, including brilliant and extensive use of seminal images, contrast of sacred *loci*, psychotherapeutic dialogue with a *potentia*, and a conversion experience in which the instincts of modesty in the lady are overcome by the sophisticated blending of appeals to reason and emotion which the nobleman invokes through the relation of the visionary experience.

From the beginning of the dialogue Andreas sprinkles the nobleman's speeches of polite seduction with seminal metaphors whose full appropriateness becomes apparent only when they appear later on transmuted in a sustained allegory. The nobleman begins by urging that love is the "omnium . . . fons et origo bonorum",[8] (*the fountain and origin of all good things*). He later states his hopes for the lady's "rorem suavitatis"[9] (*dew of happiness*) and makes a plea that she will "ad omnia peragenda bona viam aperire incognitam" (*open the unknown way to all good deeds*). She should join Love's "militia" and "curia", and dwell in his "aula". The lady in her turn does not wish to concern herself with "Veneris servituti nec amantium . . . poenis" (*servitude to Venus nor the*

[8] Andrea Capellano, *Trattato d'Amore* edited by Salvatore Battaglia (Rome, 1951), p. 94.
[9] Andrea, p. 98.

torments of lovers), and she asserts that lovers suffer from so much trouble and weariness that no one could know them "nisi experientia docet"[10] (*unless through experience*). As the argument reaches its climax, the nobleman's metaphors become so sustained as to approach allegory. "Si tali curaveritis via ambulare, intolerabilis vos poena sequetur, cui nulla similis reperitur, et quam erit recitare difficile."[11] (*If you should be so bold as to walk that path, you will meet with intolerable torments, the like of which have never been heard, and which it would be difficult to describe.*)

The lady's curiosity is so stimulated by this last remark that she asks him to describe the "poena" and the nobleman in reply breaks into a complete allegory in which he cleverly expands the seminal imagery of their conversation into the major features of his allegorical construction. First the "amoris aula" is described, with its three gates appropriate to the three classes of women who respectively are too free, or too niggardly, or keep *mesura* in the granting of their loves. Then from the static description of the palace, the nobleman proceeds to allegorical narrative. Straying from his hunting companions in an "amoenum valde locum et delectabilem",[12] he comes across a "militia" (*troops of riders*), who correspond to the three classes of ladies in the preceding allegory. A lady of the last troop befriends him, calms his fears when he learns that he has become involved with the "exercitus mortuorum" (*the hosts of the dead*), and explains that the ladies of the last troop, to which she belongs, are being punished for not granting their love to men while they were alive. He should warn all living ladies to avoid such "poena", some of which can only be known, so frightful they are, "per experientiam".[13]

He is then guided to the "amoris curia", in the region of "amoenitas", which is pleasantly watered by a "fons", so that all the ladies who have loved rightly may have enough to drink. The outer regions of "humiditas" and "siccitas" have too much and too little water respectively, and receive those who were excessive or inadequate in their acceptance of lovers on earth. But there is a "via quaedam pulcherrima" (*very delightful path*) through the unpleasant regions to the "amoenitas" at the centre.[14] The quest for authority implied in the debate is finally satisfied by the nobleman's

---

[10] Andrea, p. 100.   [11] Andrea, p. 102.
[12] Andrea, p. 106.   [13] Andrea, pp. 112, 114.
[14] Andrea, pp. 116, 118.

meeting with the Rex Amoris, who delivers to him his twelve commandments for the right guidance of ladies on earth.

Thus such images as "fons", "militia", "curia", "poena", "aula", and "via", having appeared haphazardly in the dialogue, are amplified and arranged in a logical and coherent pattern in the allegory. The consistency of the nobleman's arrangement of mutually supporting imagery parodies Christian eschatology and gives validity to each component. In particular, the lady's images are nullified by finding employment in a different sense from the one she intended. The correct service of Love is shown to lead to the life of "amoenitas", and it is the refusal to serve him properly or at all which leads to the "poena".

The dialogue as a whole offers a convincing parody of the process of conversion, in which the proselyte is overborne not so much by the validity of any particular argument as by the greater consistency and clarity of the *Weltanschauung* of his opponent. No wonder the lady can finally answer no more than

If those things which you say are true, it is a glorious thing to take part in the services of Love and very dangerous to reject his mandates. But whether what you say is true or false, the story of these terrible punishments frightens me so that I do not wish to be a stranger to Love's service; but I would be reckoned among his fellowship and would find myself a dwelling at the southern gate.[15]

She is, in fact, convinced poetically rather than rationally; allegory has proved more effective than dialogue as an instrument of argument. (The effectiveness of the appeal to her intuition, and the final logical inconsistency of her views reflect, no doubt, something of Andreas's reading of the female character.) This development from seminal image to allegory at first appears very different from anything we have seen before in this history. But the differences are not so sharp as to suggest a completely irrelevant phenomenon. All the different metaphors centre on one allegorical figure, the God of Love. Andreas's characters may be frivolous and shallow, incapable of the extreme states of tension represented in other allegories, but they nonetheless turn sustained attention to the landscapes of the inner life. Andreas here, as elsewhere, parodies the forms as well as the sentiments of more serious mental exploration.

[15] *The Art of Courtly Love* translated by Parry (New York, 1941), p. 83.

Allegory of landscape in Andreas's work is attached to a dialogue that can be called serious only in so far as a parody participates in the seriousness of what is parodied. Contemporary works such as the *Altercatio Phyllidis et Florae*, the *Altercatio Ganymedis et Helenae* and *Li Fablel dou Dieu d'Amours* depend on a conjunction of landscape and debate that takes us equally far from the philosophical dialogue. The *Altercatio Phyllidis et Florae*, a frivolous and charming poem on the relative merits of cleric and knight as lovers, may be considered a *Streitgedicht*, a form distinguishable from the allegorical dialogue in its greater emphasis on the rhetorical than the intellectual or psychological.[16] The characters merely represent points of view and do not develop under the stress of the argument; the handling of the subject is lighter in that the debaters try to score points rather than to discover or assimilate a truth, and the judges hand down a delightfully arbitrary decision to conclude the debate.

The *Altercatio Phyllidis* shows many of the formal complexities we have looked at in Andreas's fifth dialogue and elsewhere. It opens with the maiden's debate on the point at issue, and when something of a deadlock is reached, they decide to seek the advice of Cupid, whose abode turns out to be a grove, clearly a *locus amoenus*, complete with murmuring stream, soft odorous winds breathing over the banks of myrrh, sound of instruments, singing birds, and exotic revelry. The Love God refers the case to his judges, "Usus et Natura", and a speedy decision is given: "ad amorem clericus dicunt aptiorem."

Resolution of inconclusive debate by the *potentia* has been seen in Nature's judgment in the *Architrenius*, as well as in the commandments of the God of Love given to Andreas's nobleman on his visit to *Amoenitas*. The arrival at the *locus amoenus* once more heralds the solution of the problem the poem is concerned with, and similarly indicates that we are undergoing a change in the nature of the reality presented by the poem; the discussion has been lifted, almost in a Platonic sense, to the level of "ideas".

In *Li Fablel dou Dieu d'Amours* we find a further example of an

[16] Hans Walther, *Das Streitgedicht in der Lateinischen Literatur des Mittelalters* (Munich, 1920), pp. 108, 141. The *Streitgedicht* appears here in the particular form of the *question d'amour*, a variant seemingly not recognized by Walther, though it is difficult to see any significant differences between the two forms, other than the specific subject-matter of the latter.

inconclusive debate on love developing into a full-scale allegory.[17] The matter is hardly profound, but is expressed gracefully and with psychological insight. The subject reflects the exclusiveness of the erotic morality; but here the peril to love's brittle kingdom is no more serious than the boorishness of those who, by nature or mis-calculation, offend against the rules of "courtoisie". The first section of the poem relates a dream of the singing birds in the *locus amoenus*, who are now no longer singing but instead carrying on the love debate itself. The question is, what has caused love to degenerate? Is it the influence of the "villain" without courtesy? The birds reach no clear decision, but the general feeling is that love is to be considered in all circumstances an ennobling passion.

In the second part, the dreamer encounters his beloved in the same garden, but, as they start to talk lovingly to each other, the girl is carried off by a dragon and is only recovered when the dreamer goes to the palace of the God of Love and secures his intervention. The second part does not seem to have much con-nection with the first, as Langlois has noted.[18] Possibly we are to see in the dragon an allegorizing of emotional difficulties arising out of the over-boldness of the lover. In this case the dragon would be an image correspondent to that of *Daunger* in the *Roman de la Rose*, and the God of Love would correspond to the saving figure of Venus. By this interpretation the condemnation of "vilanie" in the first part may be connected with the dragon of the second. (The garden of love in the first part is forbidden to the "vilain".) The dragon would thus represent an estrangement between the lovers proceeding from a discourteous overpresumption on the part of the hero and the consequent appearance of the Lady's *Daunger*. In the *Dieu d'Amours* the debate on love acquires a less rhetorical, more psychological emphasis.

GUILLAUME DE LORRIS: THE SECRET GARDEN

Guillaume's park of Lord Mirth in the *Romance of the Rose* must be the best known of the medieval gardens of love, those richly sym-

---

[17] Edited by I. C. Lecompte, *Modern Philology* 8 (1910–11), pp. 63–86.
[18] Ernest Langlois, *Origines et Sources du Roman de la Rose* (Paris, 1891), p. 18.

bolic settings for the enactment of the private moralities of eroticism in which the age was so fertile. The idealized garden embodies (see above pp. 77–78) a harmony of city and wilderness, of reason and the non-rational faculties, and thus often constitutes the setting for the resolution of a problem involving the conflict of these elemental psychic forces. The gardens of earthly love therefore represent a deceptive or parodistic version of this harmony, an emotional satisfaction from security achieved at the expense of higher rational-moral principles rather than in concordance with them—in terms of landscape, a surrender to the wilderness in its deceptively benevolent aspect.

That the direct sources of most of the imagery in these profane gardens are Biblical may seem surprising. But the paradise garden of the first chapter of *Genesis* and the image of the *hortus conclusus* appearing in the passionate declarations of the lover in the *Song of Songs* (IV.12) embody a series of ambiguities tantalizingly appropriate for the subtle parodistic purposes of the medieval love poet. These Biblical gardens were associated respectively with prelapsarian innocence and with the purity of Christ's love for the soul, according to common allegorical exegesis. Nonetheless there were inescapable sexual associations in the Fall itself and in the modesty acquired thereby, as well as in the startlingly uninhibited erotic imagery of the *Song* (especially in the association of the *hortus conclusus* with the body of the beloved). Both gardens walled out all but the elect: redeemed souls, by some accounts, visited the earthly paradise before ascending to heaven—an association of exclusiveness easily parodied in a depiction of a snug erotic refuge walled off against jealous rivals or unbelievers according to the ethics of the god of earthly love.[19]

It might seem that actual castle gardens of the period should be considered an important influence on literary and iconographic descriptions. The typical courtly garden of the twelfth century was located in a small walled enclosure within the castle. Cultivated purely for the ordered beauty of its flowers and lawns, its enjoyment confined to the elegantly attired members of the privileged classes, it must have appeared as a haven of beauty in contrast with the country outside the castle, which was devoted to utilitarian agriculture as far as the encompassing forest or wilderness had been cleared. It is easy to forget that the attractive appearance of the

[19] Patch, *The Other World* (Harvard, 1950), pp. 136, 142, 165.

present day English countryside results from the eighteenth-century enclosure of agricultural land into park-like estates— the final metamorphosis of aristocratic landscaping in England, in which the whole countryside becomes subject to aesthetic ordering. In relation to the castle itself, the garden must also have provided a haven from the turbulence of the main hall; its development seems to have coincided with the development of private sleeping and dining rooms, which functioned similarly as refuges from the commotion and vulgarity of the retainers. In 1250, Henry III wrote to his bailiff at Woodstock with instructions "to make around about the garden of our Queen two walls, good and high, so that no one may be able to enter."[20]

Yet these real gardens should not be considered so much a source for or influence on the gardens of the poets but rather a parallel and mutually reinforcing instance of the same tendencies. The creation of a real garden is of course as extra-rational and extra-utilitarian an act as the creation of gardens of the imagination, and to be explained on basically the same psychic motivations.

The main distinguishing contributions of the poets of the gardens of love were twofold—the bold, subtle and fertile use of traditional imagery to express the sexual, social and moral dimensions of the love relationships involved; and the treatment and sometimes the resolution of the problematic relationship of the erotic *hortus conclusus* to the social and moral expectations of the world outside.

An early but particularly subtle manifestation of the tendencies we have been discussing occurs in the garden Cligés makes for his runaway mistress Fenice in Chrétien's *Cligés* (6259*ff*.). An extended love scene seems dramatically appropriate at this point of the romance, after the many hardships the lovers have had to undergo to attain bliss. The season is,

> Au renovelemant d'esté,
> Que flors et fuelles d'arbres issent,
> Et cil oisel si s'esjoissent . . .[21]

when Fenice hears the nightingale. "Le braz au flanc et l'autre au col," she tells Cligés how much she would like a garden to enjoy

[20] Evelyn Cecil, *History of Gardening in England* (London, 1910), p. 32. Sir Frank Crisp, *Medieval Gardens* (London 1924), pp. 21*ff*.
[21] *Cligés* edited by A. Micha (Paris, 1957), 6262*ff*.

herself in. (The verb she uses for enjoy, *deduire*, had also a sexual significance.) A garden has already been prepared, only enterable, it is said, through the tower in which the lovers have taken refuge. Since the spy, Bertran, later gets over the wall without entering through the tower, the symbol seems primarily phallic. The "ante" or grafted tree under which Fenice places her bed, and the pear which by falling from the tree arouses her to the presence of Bertran can also be taken in a sexual sense.[22] The morality of the lovers develops out of the circumstances of the poem into something best described as a refinement of the courtly love code, and Bertran's horror at seeing them together is a warning and a reminder to them how their actions must seem to the outside world. At this point the *hortus conclusus* becomes fully the symbol of their private morality, the ambiguities of their relationship parodistically echoing the ambiguities of innocence and sexuality of the *Song of Songs* itself. Naked lovers in a "paradise"—a fruit falls—they realize their relationship is discovered—they try desperately but unsuccessfully to conceal it. There are also conflicting undertones of the story of the Fall here, but it is an injustice to the subtleties of Chrétien's art to hear them louder than a whisper.[23]

The potentialities of the enclosed garden as a symbol of social exclusiveness were manifested most clearly in the *Dieu d'Amours* and the *Roman de la Rose*, both of which employed the figure of *Oiseuse*, "Leisure", as a porteress to guard the entrance, suggesting the unavailability of courtly love to those who lack adequate leisure and the corresponding vulnerability of the idle to the assaults of sexual temptation. The *Roman de la Rose* moreover shows the fullest development of the image of the enclosed garden to symbolize a private and limited morality.

The subtleties of Guillaume's imagery have been finely elucidated by C. S. Lewis,[24] but what has been less noted is his sophisticated development of traditional motifs to suggest something of

[22] "Et pyrus, huicque dedit materna angustia nomen" (*Architrenius* in Wright I. 294). Pyrrhus seduces the heroine of *Lydia* in a pear tree (*Poésies inédites du moyen age* edited by E. du. Méril, Paris, 1854). Among many other examples of the sexual symbolism of pears, one may cite the almost definitive instance of the lyric "I haue a newe gardyn", no. 21 in *Secular Lyrics of the XIVth and XVth Centuries* edited by Rossell Hope Robbins (Oxford, 1952).

[23] D. W. Robertson interprets this garden on more strictly "Patristic" lines in *Speculum* 26 (January 1951), pp. 39–40.

[24] *Allegory of Love*, pp. 119–20, 125–34.

the decadence of the state of mind associated with the park. The employment of *Oiseuse* as doorkeeper to this paradise (in place of some figure of the moral stature of St. Peter) is an obvious example. Less obvious is the significance of the allegorical depictions on the outside of the park wall of the qualities, ranging from Envy to Poverty, excluded from the garden. Such figures derive from the gargoyles and other apotropaic figures to be seen guarding the churches of the era from hostile psychic powers by facing them off, mirror-wise, with depictions of their own fearful resemblances. Guillaume's amusing and sophisticated use of such apotropaism reflects ironically on the charming but narrow and decadent view of reality held by the society within. "Uns vergiers," Guillaume describes the garden "ou onc n'avoit entré bergiers", (469–70); the implied social exclusiveness receives in its turn implicit rebuke from Jean de Meun's Genius (in general the soundest guide to the interpretation of Guillaume's garden) in his description of the park of the true paradise as providing pasturage for the flocks of the "sage bergier" (20401) (*The Good Shepherd*).

Guillaume above all allegorists of landscape has the power of suggesting great implications in the most casual descriptions. His effects seem effortless even in comparison with Chrétien. On first seeing the rose garden itself, the dreamer muses,

> I love well sich roses rede,
> For brode roses and open also
> Ben passed in a day or two;
> But knoppes wille [al] freshe be
> Two dayes, atte leest, or thre.
> The knoppes gretly liked me, . . . (*Romaunt*, 1680–5)[25]

In the strict allegory, the dreamer is saying no more than that he prefers his girl friends young. But we are also exposed to the mood of "Gather ye rosebuds" (an image at least as old as Ausonius) as the dreamer himself is being drawn into it. Finally, we see foreshadowed the inevitable ending of the affair, and the end of the garden itself, for this is no paradise of unfading flowers. Underlying all is a quiet mockery of a lover's hopes of earthly happiness.

While Guillaume concerns himself only indirectly with the

[25] This and subsequent verse translations of the *Roman* are by Chaucer, from F. N. Robinson's edition of *The Complete Works* (Cambridge, Mass. 1957).

deeper, the archetypal and inexpressible sides of the psychic life, he displays an acute sense of the more superficial workings of the mind. It seems not to have been remarked how the enclosed area of his garden functions as an area of temptation. The dreamer's entrance into the garden was a free and apparently reversible choice. When he sees the "roser" he is filled with "sich lust and envie" to approach it that his power of choice appears to have diminished. Finally, the arrows of the God of Love constrain him so that "Ne hadde I help of hope ne bote." Guillaume has given subtle expression to the process of succumbing to temptation. We do not regard exposing ourselves to a temptation as in any sense yielding to it, and yet without making any conscious commitment we finally discover we have apparently lost all power of free action. Within the poem itself *Resoun* makes much of this explicit in her criticism of the dreamer's activities (3220*ff.*).

In the satirical and lusty farce of "The Merchant's Tale" Chaucer made his one acknowledged use of Guillaume's garden. The lecherous old Januarie has made himself a private pleasaunce (for he liked "to lyve ful deliciously") where he sports himself with his fair young wife, May, who has given her affections, though not yet her body, to the young squire, Damyan. The garden itself was so beautiful:

> That he that wroot the Romance of the Rose
> Ne koude of it the beautee wel devyse;
> Ne Priapus ne myghte nat suffise, . . .   (IV. 2032*ff.*)[26]

And, as we learn a little later,

> This noble knyght, this Januarie the olde,
> Swich deyntee hath in it to walke and pleye,
> That he wol no wight suffren bere the keye
> Save he hymself; for of the smale wyket
> He baar alwey of silver a clyket,
> With which, whan that hym leste, he it unshette.   (IV. 2042–7)

The privacy of the garden once again suggests a private morality, for Januarie defends his uxoriousness, abhorrent as it must seem by external standards, in lengthy speeches of self-defense and self-congratulation.

[26] "The Merchant's Tale" edited by Robinson, *op. cit.*

> A man may do no synne with his wyf,
> Ne hurte hymselven with his ownene knyf; . . . (IV. 1839f.)

The sexual symbolism of the key,[27] already apparent at its first appearance, gets considerable reinforcement when, after the onset of Januarie's blindness, May arranges a duplicate for Damyan. Now all that is needed is for May to be identified with the garden, and this, by appropriate irony, is done by Januarie himself. One fine spring morning, he is persuaded to take May to the garden, but before leaving he is inspired to address her in terms of the lover of the *Song of Songs.*

> How fairer been thy brestes than is wyn!
> The gardyn is enclosed al aboute; . . . (IV. 2142–3)

Once in the garden May confesses to a woman's longing to eat pears, Damyan being ensconced up in the pear tree. (The reader will recall a similar symbolic use of the pear tree in *Cligés,* see p. 101 above.) As soon as May is up the tree, Damyan "sodeynly" goes to work. The symbolic mechanism of the plot stands revealed. Priapus, in the person of the taciturn young page, whose sexual passion has been adulterous, intense, but not particularly courtly, triumphs over the loquacious husband, the self-proclaimed idyllic lover, who has attempted, against all doctrine, religious or courtly, to make his marriage into a "rose garden". We have seen, in fact, the acting out of the implications of Januarie's motives in taking a wife, as he expressed them at the opening of the poem.

> "For wedlok is so esy and so clene,
> That in this world it is a paradys . . ."
> And namely whan a man is oold and hoor,
> Thanne is a wyf the fruyt of his tresor. (IV. 1264–70)

We have seen how the medieval allegorist frequently develops a seminal image analytically into a complete allegorical situation. Here Chaucer has made a brilliant ironical use of this procedure in a poem which is technically not allegorical at all.

Not all representations of private moralities use such techniques and motifs. The "Chapel of Love" in the grotto of Gottfried von

---

[27] *Cf.* for example, the "Dyonea clavis" in the quotation from Alan of Lille on p. 49, above.

Strassburg's *Tristan*, with its parody of religious imagery, represents the private ethos behind the actions of the lovers in explicit and detailed allegory. But the privacy here is conveyed by the isolation rather than the enclosure of the grotto, and appropriately so since the lovers are seen as quite isolated from the sympathy of the world in their conduct, not merely as following the morality of an exclusive minority. So too, with similar appropriateness, Fenice's garden in *Cligés* is isolated and secret, as well as enclosed. In Andreas's *Art of Love* we twice find Love's kingdom on the "other side of the forest", once as a parody of the landscape of the rewards and punishments of the afterlife, once masquerading as the court of King Arthur.[28] Here again, isolation is the principal barrier, though the Knight of Britain has also to pass over a well-defended "perilous bridge" on his way to Arthur's court.

The enclosed garden thus became for a number of reasons the natural symbol of the private morality of an exclusive class, though allegorical *loci*, separated from normal life by some form of barrier, were also employed for this purpose. Such gardens through their Biblical and Patristic associations, were particularly suited for parodying the beliefs and institutions of the Church and the parody in its turn served to define and to model the private morality. At the same time the parody could express the poet's doubts, slight or strong, about the final validity of such moralities. Allegorists were also able to find in the garden a wealth of priapic associations which could be drawn on to symbolize the erotic aspects of the courtly way of life. Hence the particular appropriateness to the allegorist of the gardens in *Genesis* and the *Song of Songs* with their combined spiritual and erotic overtones.

JEAN'S "ROMAN": THE GARDEN INVADED

In the first part of the *Roman de la Rose* we saw the garden imagery conveying the atmosphere and the psychological development of a refined love affair. In his continuation Jean de Meun further developed the possibilities of the genre, if he did not in fact overload it, by bringing into the poem the *potentiae*, dialogues, and

[28] Parry, *The Art of Courtly Love*, 74ff., 177ff.

landscapes of the philosophical epic in the style of Alan of Lille or Jean de Hanville. This broadening and deepening of the poem was not so alien to Guillaume's intention as sometimes implied. Jean's paradise garden is brilliantly contrasted with the garden of the courtly life, but it should be noted that Guillaume, in his unobtrusive way, had already inserted into the poem something of an antithesis to the Rose Garden. After the dreamer has been driven away from the *roser* by *Daunger*, *Resoun* decides to pay him a visit.

> A long while stod I in that stat,
> Til that me saugh so mad and mat
> The lady of the highe ward,
> Which from hir tour lokide thiderward.
> Resoun men clepe that lady,
> Which from hir tour delyverly
> Com doun to me, withouten mor. . . .

> "Thou hast bought deere the tyme of May,
> That made thyn herte mery to be.
> In yvell tyme thou wentist to see
> The gardyn, . . ."   (3189–95, 3222–5)

Though the dreamer, unlike Boethius, has not recognized the perils of his situation, we know that the tower overtops the wall, and from afar, dominates the scene in the garden. Mark in Gottfried's *Tristan*, Bertran in *Cligés*, and the dragon in the *Dieu d'Amours* all violate Love's *hortus conclusus*, but they are natural enemies of love and as much part of its pattern as *Daunger* in the *Roman*. *Resoun* is outside the pattern; or to put it another way, she is an internal rather than an external impediment to the progress of the affair, and thus the more redoubtable an adversary. Ultimately she will have to be reconciled if the garden is to survive.

Previously allegorists of the "School of Chartres" had approached the problems of human sexuality from a philosophical standpoint; now Guillaume in return is approaching the demands of the ethical life from the secular, the profane, and specifically the courtly and amorous standpoint. The "given" is the sexual urge. Jean de Meun extends but does not radically alter Guillaume's method in this respect. Both methods have their particular advantages, but Guillaume and Jean start from a point more general to human experience.

In Jean de Meun's continuation of the poem, the potentialities of the garden as an allegorical device are so neglected that it becomes a half-forgotten backdrop for the dialogues, monologues and somewhat inappropriately staged psychomachia that make up the bulk of his contribution. On the whole, therefore, Jean hardly succeeds in turning the juxtaposition of landscape and dialogue he inherited to much profit. Dialogue almost entirely supplants the allegory of landscape and, where the latter does appear, it is not often effectively used. The resolution of the poem, for example, is expressed in terms of landscape—the final storming of the Castle of the Rose, but this solution signifies little in terms of the dialogue.

The great exception to these strictures on Jean's failure to use the allegorical potentialities he inherited is his description of the paradisal Park of the Good Shepherd, which he contrasts explicitly and in considerable detail with Guillaume's garden of the courtly life. This contrast of gardens, as C. S. Lewis has shown, is one of Jean's most effective contributions to the poem. Lewis himself would regard it as unintegrated to the poem as a whole; like most of Jean's writing, it "reads best in quotation".[29] Alan Gunn, in his work on the poem *The Mirror of Love*, on the other hand argues generally for the coherence of Jean's part of the poem as an organized and sustained argument on the nature of love.[30] An examination of the relationship of the Good Park to the dialogue in which it stands may throw some light also on this wider question.

Genius's sermon to the barons, in which the description of the park occurs, turns out to be an exhortation to obey Nature's command to keep the earth populated by vigorous and frequent sexual intercourse. That admission to the good park is the reward for such conduct is at first somewhat surprising. The sermon frequently sounds like an amusing parody, and the description of the park seems too sublime for its context. But Genius, "genial" in the modern sense as his sermon may be at times, is invested with serious responsibilities for the reproductive functions and is at this point, moreover, clothed in a chasuble supplied to him by Cupid; in other words he is speaking in connection with his particular duty to give counsel to lovers. Nor, as Genius explains at the end of his sermon, is a healthy attitude towards sex the only virtue required for entrance to the park; one should return the goods of others, avoid

[29] *Allegory of Love*, pp. 152ff.
[30] Alan Gunn, *The Mirror of Love* (Lubbock, Texas, 1952).

being concerned in killing, be pure of hands and mouth, be loyal and merciful:

> E se de l'autrui riens avez,
> Rendez le, se vous le savez, . . .
> D'ocision nus ne s'aprouche,
> Netes aiez e mains e bouche;
> Seiez leial, seiez piteus,
> Lors ireiz ou champ deliteus, . . .[31]

It is also our duty to keep the more conventional commandments. Complaint about the wickedness of man has been the *leitmotiv* of Nature's lengthy confession to Genius which precedes the sermon, so the caution seems very much in place. Man's natural instincts toward evil, Nature asserted, may be corrected by Reason, if one will have faith in her:

> Car, quant de sa propre nature,
> Contre bien e contre dreiture
> Se veaut on ou fame atourner,
> Raison l'en peut bien destourner,
> Pour qu'il la creie seulement; . . . (17087–91)

Thus Genius's exhortation to fecundity can be regarded as an appropriate synecdoche of a general exhortation that lovers should follow virtue. In fact Jean is using a sexual synecdoche for virtue in precisely the fashion that his master Alan of Lille used a sexual synecdoche for vice.

Nonetheless, as soon as Genius has vanished from the scene, Venus, who has been assisting him in inflaming the ardour of the barons with the *cierge*, makes clear her hostility to Reason in an abusive speech of defiance to her daughter, Shame, who is among the defenders of the Rose Castle.

> Certes, Honte, ja n'amerai
> Ne vous ne Raison vostre mere,
> Qui tant est aus amanz amere.
> Qui vostre mere e vous crerait
> Jamais par amour n'amerait. (20778–82)

---

[31] *Roman de La Rose* edited by Langlois (Paris, 1914–24), 20639*ff.*

The lover moreover, enjoying "les baisiers savoureus" after the fall of the castle, thanks Venus and the God of Love ten or twenty times.

> Mais de Raison ne me souvint,
> Qui tant en mei gasta de peine.[32]

I conclude that Jean's account of the Good Park fits very well into its immediate setting, Genius's sermon, showing as it does the rewards of honest copulation for the purpose of procreation, as opposed to the sterile love associated with the Rose Garden.[33] But Reason, Nature, and Venus are left in a state of disharmony, and the poet does not seem to acknowledge the need to say anything clear about their interrelationships.[34] The solution of the *Architrenius*, the principle of *moderantia* as reconciling Venus and Nature, is neglected: Jean seems to have no more taste for moderation than for consistency. The formulation of the moment suffices. The same disharmony is reflected in the landscapes. The Park of the Good Shepherd stands finally in no clear relationship to the Rose Garden, for Genius assists very actively in the assault on the Castle of the Rose, just after comparing the Rose Garden so slightingly to the Good Park. The apparent ambiguity of this is not resolved. He seems to have forgotten, moreover, that he is giving his sermon in the very garden he is attacking. The landscape and ← the dialogue are no longer in harmony.

Jean's failure to make a clear statement concerning the hierarchical relationships of his *potentiae* would have almost fatally blemished a visionary allegory in the strict Chartrian mode. In the *Roman*, however, it is not so much a blemish as an indication of the accuracy with which Jean reflects the state of mind of his dreaming hero. While the dreamer experiences a certain psychic shock when he first encounters the arrows of the God of Love, he never

---

[32] *Roman* 21760ff. He never once thought of Reason who had given him so much trouble.

[33] *Cf.* the speech of *Raison*, 4385ff.

[34] *Cf.* Alan Gunn, *The Mirror of Love*, p. 500. "Something, then, is left unresolved and unintegrated at the close of the work. The scheme of values represented in Raison's discourse, does not, one must admit, fit into the essentially comic and life-embracing world of Amis, Amors, La Vieille, Nature, and Genius." Rosemond Tuve, on the other hand sweeps away the whole problem of these discrepancies by interpreting Nature and Genius as satirical portraits whose doctrines are intended to be absurdly unacceptable (*Allegorical Imagery*, Princeton, 1966, pp. 245ff.).

undergoes anything comparable in depth to the spiritual crises of the heroes of the Chartrian allegories, and thus never feels the urgency of their desire for a vision of the ultimate truth concerning their spiritual condition. His quest consequently tends to peter out into diversion and irrelevance: the *potentiae*, freed from the dreamer's anguished demand for personal assistance and enlightenment, may discourse on any subject that comes into their heads, as they notoriously do, for many thousands of lines. From the literary point of view the results seem shapeless and unorganized, and I do not think it possible to defend Jean by showing an articulate schema underneath the apparent confusion, as Mr. Gunn has heroically attempted to do. Rather, the true defence is that where the Chartrians depicted high spiritual pilgrimage, Jean gives us a pretty fair representation of the inner lives of the rest of us, shapeless and inconsistently motivated as they are. This is the way most of us live, and to complain of his unwillingness or inability to give an adequate structure to his poem is in a sense to complain of his excessive fidelity in representing the human condition. Nonetheless, the need remained for a definite statement concerning the right relationships of the *potentiae* of love, and Jean's provocative abstention from such a formulation was to constitute a recurrent challenge to his successors.

7

Dante

IN the *Commedia*, all the potentialities and developments of medieval allegory that we have been tracing are brought to their highest point of realization. The symbolic structure is the most comprehensive and sophisticated of any medieval allegory, embodying the development of the *imagines* from the earliest apprehensible stage of psychological and spiritual development to the most advanced and profound. At the same time, the visionary dialogues of the poem provide a searching rational commentary on this evolution of the symbolic structure. The general tendency of Dante's mind exemplifies in the highest degree the typically medieval desire to accept and to harmonize all modes of thought and experience: no symbolic structure is repudiated as such, nor even any mode of thought; rather they are brought together in a vast unified scheme which relates them to one central and all-encompassing reality.[1] The comprehensiveness of the vision, moreover, enables Dante to give more complete and satisfying answers to the intellectual, spiritual and technical problems inherent in the visionary allegories of his predecessors.

THE "SELVA SELVAGGIA"

Etienne Gilson, in his masterly study, *Dante and Philosophy* (New York, 1962), distinguishes two styles or types of symbol in the

[1] *Cf.* W. H. Auden's seminal comment: "In the supreme master of the dream, Dante, we find simultaneously an inexhaustible flow of images of the profoundest resonance and a meticulous logical and mathematical structure which even dictates the number of verses" (Introduction to *The Visionary Novels of George Macdonald*, New York, 1954, p. vi). For an opposite interpretation and a negative consideration of allegory, see the Italian romantic criticism and especially: Francesco De Sanctis, *Lezioni sulla Divina Commedia* (Bari, 1955), pp. 45–49.

Commedia—one, complex, exemplified by such persons of the drama as Vergil, Beatrice and Dante himself, "primarily symbolic of what they are"; the other, the non-human symbols, being "simple", mere "poetical fancies". Gilson particularly singles out for illustration of the latter certain constituents of the landscape of the first canto, such as the dark forest, the sun, the beautiful mountain, the fierce beasts (pp. 291–2).

But it is difficult to see how the *selva oscura* and its animals can be termed simple images, when one considers their immensely complex development since the beginnings of recorded human experience. We have previously touched on some interpretations of these images in discussing the psychology of landscape and have seen how the struggle of ancient man to overcome his fears of the wilderness manifested itself in mythical battles between heroes and monsters. We have also seen how with the coming of the Christian era the fear of monsters becomes separated from the horror of sin, with a consequent fading of the power of the monster figure to terrify, a process we have seen with particular clarity in Prudentius' *Psychomachia*.

The *Commedia*, therefore, opens with a restatement of the eternal conflict of man and monster appropriate to the psychological state of Dante as an individual, and, in a wider sense, as representative of his time and circumstances, one living in a part of Christendom distant from the frontiers and the wilderness. The animals of the *selva oscura* are no Grendels; they represent known species, and they have the power to hinder and frighten the poet rather than to destroy him. In terms of modern psychology, certain not fully identified forces of his subconscious mind are powerful enough to prevent his attaining the state of salvation, or the inner peace that he desires, but are not powerful enough to overthrow his reason altogether.

The sun and the delectable mountain are also important constituents of the opening of the poem, and together these "simple" symbols constitute a scene which shows the state of mind of a man open to the possibilities of Christian salvation, but kept from salvation by the sinfulness within him. We must notice that all the imagery here is basically pre-Christian. As we shall see in further detail later, so far as the development of imagery is concerned the process of salvation depicted in the *Commedia* consists of an allegorical analysis of the basic images of the prologue, in terms of the much more complex and developed imagery of the rest of the poem. The three beasts will prove to correspond to the various divisions of the sins in the Inferno, the delectable mountain to Mount Purgatory, and the sun itself to the final vision of the Celestial Paradise. In each case a seemingly simple pre-Christian image is developed and analysed in great detail in terms of explicitly Christian imagery, to reveal its potential complexity.

On the conscious level of allegory proper, Dante must have thought of himself as drawing this pre-Christian imagery from classical and Biblical sources. The *selva oscura* is no doubt to be connected with the dark forests associated with the underworld in *Aeneid* VI—an association confirmed in such works as Seneca's *Oedipus Rex* (III.530*ff.*), and Lucan's *Pharsalia* (VI.642*ff.*). The beasts get their particular association with sin from the verses in *Jeremiah* (v.6):

> Idcirco percussit eos leo de silva
> lupus ad vesperam vastavit eos;
> pardus vigilans super civitates eorum:
> omnis qui egressus fuerit ex eis capietur,
> quia multiplicae sunt praevaricationes eorum,
> confortae sunt aversiones eorum.

> *Wherefore a lion out of the forest shall slay them,*
> *and a wolf of the evenings shall spoil them,*
> *a leopard shall watch over their cities:*
> *every one that goeth out thence*
> *shall be torn in pieces:*
> *because their transgressions are many,*
> *and their backslidings are increased.*

These animals, as one might expect, did not escape varied Patristic and medieval exegesis; Jerome, for example, saw them as respectively the three kingdoms of the Babylonians, Persians, and of Alexander. However, Garnerus of St. Victor has interpretations more relevant to our purposes, when he writes concerning *Bestiae* (*Patrologia Latina* volumn 193, column 197):

Bestiae nomine mens irrationabilis designatur, sicut per Moysen dicitur: *Bestia, si tetigerit montem, lapidabitur* [*Exodus* XIX.12]. Mons quippe est altitudo contemplationis; bestia vero, mens irrationabilis. Bestia ergo montem tangit, cum mens irrationabilibus desideriis subdita, ad contemplationis alta se erigit. Sed lapidibus percutitur, quia summa non sustinens ipsis superni ponderis ictibus necatur.

By the name "beast" is meant the irrational mind, as it is declared through Moses: If a beast set foot on the mountain, he will be stoned to death. *[Exodus* XIX.12]. *For the mountain is properly the loftiness of contemplation, and the beast the irrational mind. The beast sets foot on the mountain then, when the mind subject to irrational desires sets itself to attain the heights of contemplation. But it is struck by stones, for, unable to reach the summit, it perishes by these blows of celestial force.*

We have here an allegory remarkably similar in essentials to the treatment of the theme of the mountain in the opening scene of the *Commedia*. In both the ancient taboo of the holy mountain is transformed into an allegory of the spiritual life. But Garnerus has such a sense of the internal nature of the forces represented by the *Bestiae* of the wilderness that in his little allegory the animals represent purely mental forces, and are unable to approach the heights of holy contemplation; whereas in the *Commedia* the animals are in the fullest sense symbolic *imagines* and are experienced entirely as external forces within the poet's spiritual world: thus they are depicted in the active role of preventing the poet from ascending the mountain.

The three beasts are associated with the forest, as well as the hill an association that Dante may have considered not only in his poetic imagination but also through the eyes of the commentators. Very likely he was acquainted with Bernardus Sylvestris's commentary on the *Aeneid* in which the beasts and the forest are interpreted as follows:

in silvam in collectionem temporalium bonum, umbrosam et inviam quia non est nisi umbra. *Antiquam* ab initio temporis natam *Stabula* mansiones fumo vitiorum immundas *alta* elationem intuentia *ferarum* i.e. hominum in naturam vitio transformatorum. Vocat enim philosophia luxuriosos sues, fraudulentos vulpes, garrulos canes, truculentos leones, iracundos apros, rapaces lupos, torpentes asinos. Hi omnes temporalia bona inhabitant sicut econtra "bonorum conversio in celis est."[2]

[2] *Commentum Bernardi Silvestris super sex libros Eneidos Vergilii* nunc primum edidit Guilelmus Riedel (Gryphiswaldae, 1924), p. 62 (on *Aeneid* VI.179). *Cf.* E. M. W. Tillyard's remarks on the *Aeneid* passage in *Poetry: Direct and Oblique* (London, 1945), p. 26.

Into the forest—*into the accumulation of temporal goods, shadowy and trackless because it is itself no more than shadow.* Ancient—*born at the beginning of time;* lairs—*habitations defiled by the fumes of vice;* lofty— *busily seeking advancement;* beasts—*that is, men transformed in their very nature by vice. For philosophy calls the lustful pigs, the deceitful foxes, the gossiping dogs, the surly lions, the wrathful boars, the greedy wolves, the sluggardly asses. All of these dwell among temporal goods, just as, on the other hand, "the occupation of the just is in Heaven."*

Bernardus' pungent and ingenious allegorization can be justified mythologically by appeal to Circe's transformations of men into beasts in accordance with their vices. But he seems uninterested in (or perhaps shrinks from) the awe of the ancient wilderness that Vergil's lines express, an awe that is captured and intensified in the Dantean *amara* and *paura*. Such an entry into the *silva antiqua* as Vergil describes demands more emotional response than Bernardus seems prepared to allow.

The *dilettoso monte* may be primarily associated with the Sinai of *Exodus* XIX and with the *montem domini* of the twenty-third psalm. Behind these Biblical associations lies a whole body of feeling about the sacredness of mountains, some of which would be accessible to Dante through the frequent references to Zion as the holy hill of the Lord in both Old and New Testaments, and the pagan associations of Olympus and Helicon. So far as specific allegorical interpretation is concerned, though he may not have encountered Garnerus of St. Victor, he may well have come across such a passage as the more famous Richard of St. Victor's allegorizing of the mountain in the seventy-fifth chapter of the *Benjamin Minor* (*Patrologia Latina* volume 196, column 54):

Animus qui ad scientiae altitudinem nititur ascendere, primum et principale sit ei studium seipsum cognoscere. Magna altitudo scientiae seipsum perfecte cognovisse. Mons magnus et altus, plena cognitio rationalis spiritus. Omnium mundanarum scientiarum cacumina mons iste transcendit, omnem philosophiam, omnem mundi scientiam ab alto despicit. Quid tale Aristoteles, quid tale Plato invenit, quid tanta philosophorum turba, tale invenire potuit? . . . Hic defecerunt scrutantes scrutinio. Hic, inquam, defecerunt, et hunc in montem minime ascendere poterant.

Let the soul which strives to rise to the loftiness of knowledge take as its first and principal study to know itself. For the highest peak of knowledge

*is perfect knowledge of one's self. A great and lofty mountain is the full
understanding of a rational soul. This mountain rises above all the peaks of
the earthly sciences, and looks down from on high on all philosophy, all
earthly knowledge. Could Aristotle, or Plato, or the mighty throng of the
philosophers find anything such as this? . . . Here the searchers fell short
in their search; here, I say, they fell short and were wholly unable to ascend
the mountain.*

In this respect of expanding upon and making, as it were, an
allegorical analysis of ancient sacred texts, the method of the poem
approaches that of the conventional allegorical commentary of the
patristic Biblical exegete. While any attempt to link Dante's
imagery with closeness and exactitude to the fourfold method of
conventional Biblical interpretation tends to break down in detail,
there will usually be found not only much correspondence in individual particulars, as in the above examples, but also, what is far
more significant, a kind of poetic analysis of the ancient imagery
which will enormously expand and develop the potential meanings
within it. This is of course similar to the method of non-poetical
exegesis, the two having in common a technique of analysis and
amplification by means of allegory. Dantean allegory, however,
recreates a total situation that includes its primitive and symbolic
as well as the later, more rational, allegorical aspects. The typical
exegete sees no more than an over-intellectualized and fragmentary
glimpse of the whole. Dante's use of these ancient images is no mere
shading in of ancient and impressive associations, but a sustained
re-creation of the emotional and psychic as well as intellectual
power of these images for his contemporaries. Though we have
recently gained many insights into biological evolution, we seem to
have lost Dante's sense of an evolution of imagery.

We shall find therefore that the landscape of the opening of the
Commedia comprises a host of seminal images unique in their richness and subtlety of development. In addition to the major images
which we have already discussed, the metaphors of the first canto
embody a number of minor images of landscape, which have a
similar seminal function. "La . . . via . . . smarrita", "La
paura . . . nel lago del cor", the escape "del pelago alla riva",
"lo passo, che non lasciò giammai persona viva", "la piaggia diserta", the "città" of the "Imperador", and "la porta di San Pietro",
among others, will all appear again, in diverse expanded forms

which will through analysis and polarization enlarge our comprehension of the significance of the seminal images and their place in the universal scheme of things.

THE VERGILIAN CATEGORIES

Having distinguished two different aspects of the *imagines* of the opening landscapes—the symbolic and the allegorical—we must nonetheless insist that while the symbolic aspects are immediately presented by the poet, the allegorical associations are so far only potential, and we are not entitled to actualize them until the poet gives the word. Still less are we entitled to make speculative associations of these images with such random biographical motifs as Dante's exile, his disillusion with philosophy, or Florentine politics. The allegorical values, like the symbolic, must be established in the immediate context by such means as explicit interpretation or significant similarities and contrasts with other images to which the reader may be expected to respond. Nor should we fall into the error of believing that such explication, rational or imagistic, explains away the original symbolism; rather, it creates new dimensions.

The world of primordial consciousness represented by this landscape contains nothing by which it may be interpreted. There are no points of orientation apart from the sun and the sacred mountain denied to Dante by the beasts.[3] From this primeval terror of the desert and meaninglessness there comes a figure, a shade to rescue him—the figure of Vergil, who will bring meaning and orientation into the desert. We may be reminded of Gilson's wise but enigmatic description of the persons of the *Commedia* as "symbolic of what they are". Vergil is not "Reason" as such—for Dante had ample precedent for calling him by such a name if this was his intention, and none for writing a trivial *roman à clef*. Rather, Vergil is the first man's psychic evolution, at least to Dante's knowledge, to descend into the underworld and plant the flag of rational comprehension in that place of archetypal darkness and confusion.

[3] The importance of orientation and a "world centre" for the primitive mind is discussed by Mircea Eliade in *The Sacred and the Profane* (New York, 1961), pp. 32ff.

This was done, moreover, not as in the Egyptian Book of the Dead, or in the Orphic mysteries, to enable the disembodied soul to find the right way to his eternal rest, but rather to enable the hero to live a life on earth with greater understanding and spiritual strength. Vergil embodies in this respect a type of heroic rationality which is adequate for intellectual comprehension (though not full mastery) of the sins of the underworld and the painful acquisition of human virtue, but which is not yet touched by divine grace. The figure of Vergil, like all other major figures in the poem, is enormously enriched by the heritage of personification allegory that Dante was able to draw upon; but this does not justify us in turning these figures into disguised personifications.

The first psychological impact of Vergil on the state of mind of the poet is depicted with great subtlety and delicacy. The landscape imagery which previous to their encounter had reflected only the confusion of the primal wilderness now begins in the first dialogue of the poets to assume shape and identity, with talk of the *città*, and the *porta di San Pietro*. The canto concludes with the two poets taking the first steps on their long way, and immediately with the opening of the second canto we understand that the nature of reality has changed for Dante; he becomes aware of a new kind of loneliness:

> Lo giorno se n'andava, e l'aer bruno
> toglieva gli animai, che sono in terra,
> dalle fatiche loro; ed io sol uno. . . .
> *Inferno* II.1–3

The day was departing and the brown air taking the beasts that dwell on earth from their labours, and I, all alone, . . .

In going with Vergil, Dante has severed himself from the natural world, and immediately feels the *angst* of a man between two worlds—fleeing but not yet emotionally severed from the natural, nor sensing himself capable of sustaining "la guerra sì del cammino" of the spiritual world.[4] In the important dialogue with Vergil which occupies the second canto he has to learn that while he cannot enter, as a major pagan hero or Christian saint, in his own

[4] For recognition of the feeling of loneliness and severance in souls far away from their native land, see: Attilio Momigliano, *Dante, Manzoni, Verga* (Messina, 1944), p. 10.

right, he is under the protection of a special, unearned, divine grace, manifested in Beatrice's plea to Vergil to come to the aid of the imperilled poet.[5] The action of the dialogue is, as often, juxtaposed against a parallel action of symbolic-mythical significance, in this case the poet's physical hesitation at the portals of hell. On seeing the dreadful "parole di colore oscuro" inscribed above hell-gate, he exclaims, with magnificent ambiguity, "Maestro, il senso lor m'e duro", where we may take *duro* to indicate "harsh" or "bitter", as well as "difficult to understand", just as *oscuro* suggests darkness as well as mystery. But Vergil, comprehending the ambiguity, calls upon him to leave behind him not *speranza* but *sospetto*[6] and *viltà* (mistrust and cowardice) and sweeps him unresisting through the gate, now convinced both intellectually and emotionally of his fitness to enter the underworld.

The episode as a whole constitutes an excellent example of the way medieval allegory elaborates on and brings out in rational form the potential significances of a situation characteristic of a mythical stage of culture. Involved in the incident, one which was clearly very much alive to Dante, are the awe, the mingled repulsion and attraction of the sacred place, and in particular the instinctive fear of crossing its boundaries. Some primitive manifestations of this instinct are described in the second chapter of Arnold van Gennep's *Rites of Passage*, where he is concerned with the magico-religious taboos on crossing frontiers among pre-literate peoples. The natural boundary of a semi-civilized tribe may be a "sacred rock, tree, river, or lake, which cannot be crossed . . . without the risk of supernatural sanctions. . . . More often the boundary is marked by an object—a stake, portal, or upright rock . . . —whose installation at that particular spot has been accompanied by rites of consecration." A stranger crossing this boundary "commits a sacrilege analogous to a profane person's entrance into a sacred forest or temple." The tribal areas are cut off from each other by neutral zones.

Because of the pivoting of sacredness, the territories on either side of the neutral zone are sacred in relation to whoever is in the zone, but the

---

[5] Contrast Aeneas's confidence in his right to make the descent to the underworld shown in *Aeneid* VI.122–4, a confidence echoed by his guide, the Sibyl, in VI.403–4.

[6] *Sospetto* is used in similar circumstances with a similar meaning in *Inferno* IX.51.

zone, in turn, is sacred for the inhabitants of the adjacent territories. Whoever passes from one to the other finds himself physically and magico-religiously in a special situation for a certain length of time; he wavers between two worlds.[7]

Van Gennep's investigations to a degree enable us to put ourselves in the mental position of the primitive whose places of local geography are identifiable with the places of his soul, and thus to sympathize more fully with the allegorical methods used by Dante and other medieval poets. They draw not upon artificial or fancifully created conventions but upon primitive patterns of the mind which have been obscured, but not totally obliterated, by the sophistications of civilization, whether medieval or modern.

As we look at later developments of barrier symbolisms, we see that the sacred objects used to mark the portal or threshold frequently appear in the form of inscriptions from sacred texts, as a society becomes literate. Naturally, too, these sacred barriers become particularly attached to beliefs about the entrance to the regions of the dead.[8] The crossing of the sacred threshold is often accompanied by religious rites. In pagan religions of the west, none of these threshold ceremonies was more solemn or intensive than that associated with the crossing of the most sacred of all portals, the gate of the underworld. Dante had in his mind at this time, it is clear, every detail of Aeneas's descent to the underworld, but we may notice that while Aeneas descends into Hades in his own right, (and undergoes numerous ceremonies of propitiation of the underworld gods in order to do so), the Dante and Vergil of the *Commedia*, though much humbler in their pretensions than Aeneas, naturally make no such attempt at propitiation. The rulers of the underworld had since Aeneas's day lost at the "Harrowing of Hell" whatever independent power had once been theirs. In terms of the development of the western psyche we can see that the myth marked the final subjection of the underworld to a monotheistic skygod—the end of an era in which the powers of sky and

---

[7] *The Rites of Passage* translated by Vizedom (Chicago, 1960), pp. 15–18.

[8] For references to apotropaic inscriptions to ward off evil spirits from the gates, see Hastings's *Encyclopedia of Religion and Ethics* IV, p. 850, and for references to gates of the underworld, IV, p. 851. See also H. C. Trumbull, *The Threshold Covenant* (New York, 1906), for ceremonies connected with sacred gates.

chthonic deities were roughly equal. In a rough modern translation, the powers of the rational and intuitive mind would now dominate rather than equipoise the darker and more primitive instincts. Medieval allegory was thus itself one method by which the hegemony of the higher mental powers was further extended over the powers of darkness—the *id*, if you will. The entry of Dante into the underworld is in psychological time a highly important event, as representing the point of greatest rational control over the dark powers, before they become so weakened as to be first patronized (as in *Paradise Lost*) and then finally ignored.

This control is primarily effected on the symbolic level by means of the barrier, which is synonymous on the rational level with the category.[9] The first of these barriers is the sacred gate which, as we have seen, is also the first consciously recognized barrier/category in man's psychological development; we are at the start of man's psychic history. Once through the barrier, we enter into the world of categories. The first category, the nameless vestibule of the morally neutral, disposes of those who have evaded all moral categorization; appropriately, no group in hell is the subject of deeper scorn. And so the afterworlds are reduced to a final order; and the reader, participating imaginatively in the process, is enabled to map hell, that is, to conquer the underworld—whose essence is chaos—for himself. (We should remember that the modern habit of reading the *Commedia* with the aid of maps and notes supplied by conscientious editors somewhat blurs the basic spiritual-psychological value of the poem for the participating reader—this opportunity of imposing order on the underworld for himself.)

As we move through the afterworlds, we find not only that the scheme of categorization encompasses moral judgments as a basis for classifying men in ideal landscapes, but that every type of human attitude, temperament and event is displayed in ordered

[9] The Greek *nomos* and the Latin *divisio* still preserve something of the barrier/category ambiguity. *Nomos* can indicate a tract of or division of land, as well as a custom, law, statute or decision. *Divisio* can refer to a division dividing up an area of land as well as to analysis of a topic. The barrier is not, of course, the only symbol of categorization; any form of contrast or polarization of images will normally imply categorizing. *Cf.* Edmund Leach's comments in "Levi-Strauss in the Garden of Eden: An Examination of some recent developments in the analysis of myth", *Transactions of the New York Academy of Sciences* (February 1961), especially p. 394.

succession, creating a kind of counterpoint to the basic moral classification. Dante creates the most ambitious of all allegorical *summa*: where Bernardus Sylvestris and Alan of Lille sought to represent the creation-categorization of the universe and man in terms of universals and essences, where Spenser attempted to represent the moral life of man experientially, Dante combines both the essential and the particularistic views of the physical and moral worlds into one harmonious representation of the micro- and macrocosmic universe.

THE REDEMPTION OF IMAGES

The allegorical structure of the *Commedia*, then, makes manifest the dynamic intellectual impetus that underlies the Aristotelian-Thomistic categorical method. While the total scope of material categorized is no less comprehensive than that of Aristotle or Thomas, our particular concern here is with Dante's images and their categorization. Nonetheless, so extensive and complex is his development of psychic landscapes of the *Commedia* from the seminal images already identified in the first canto that no more than a few examples must suffice here.[10]

The image of primary experience of the external world, for Dante, as for Vergil and indeed for western man in general, is that of the *selva oscura*. In its appearance in the first canto, the image is by no means a clear one: indeed the poet admits how difficult the *selva* is to describe, and confines himself to a few generic adjectives —"selvaggia ed aspra e forte"—nor is the *selva* distinguished very clearly from the "piaggia diserta"[11] (*the desert strand*). The obscurity of the terrain is highly appropriate; by its very nature the primary image should be difficult to discern clearly, reflecting as it does the mental condition of a man lost in the wilderness. Nonetheless the poet makes one definite if enigmatic statement about the

[10] The manner of Dante's development of seminal imagery into allegory is elucidated (though not examined in detail) by Charles Singleton in "Allegory", *Essays on Dante* edited by Mark Musa (Indiana, 1964), pp. 60–61.

[11] For general discussion of the *selva*, see pp. 75–7 above. For analysis of the shifting levels of reality in the opening cantos of "the Anteinferno" see Singleton's "Allegory", especially pp. 58–9.

wood, that so bitter was his fear "che poco è più morte", and yet, to tell of the good that he found there, he will relate the other things he discerned:

> ma per trattar del ben ch' i'vi trovai,
> dirò dell' altre cose, ch' io v'ho scorte.

In an immediate sense, the *ben* is no doubt his meeting with Vergil and learning of his saving mission. But a closer attention to the text suggests a further interpretation. There was actual good in the *selva*, and to clarify what it was, he will tell us of the other things that he discerned there. The phrase *altre cose* would seem to refer to more than the encounter with Vergil, perhaps to the images of the first canto in their seminal aspect. Through their elucidation by categorical analysis into unfavourable and favourable elements for rejection or acceptance, he will discover the *ben*, the ultimate good inherent in the celestial archetypes from which all manifestations of the images ultimately proceed.

The next manifestation of the *selva*, the wood of the suicides in the seventh circle of the Inferno, on the other hand, is described with a remorseless clarity of detail.

> Non frondi verdi, ma di color fosco;
> non rami schietti, ma nodosi e involti;
> non pomi v'eran, ma stecchi con tosco. (XIII.4–6)

Here the forest has lost its obscurity, for we are facing directly the menace that appeared to be lurking behind the *selva oscura*, and which caused Dante's original overwhelming *paura*. While this infernal manifestation of the forest is horrifyingly corrupted and desolate, it does not stimulate the same terror of the unknown as before, for, as we have seen, identification and confrontation of what underlies the feeling of menace destroys the terror. We are left with only the horror of the sinful aspect of the original terror, now identifiable as the sin of self-destruction. As in Prudentius's *Psychomachia*, but with infinitely greater subtlety in use of imagery and corresponding psychological insight, we have achieved a separation of the sense of sin from the sense of the nameless underworld terror. Once more, we have participated in a re-enactment of a critical phase of man's spiritual and psychological history.

Accordingly, the geography of this manifestation of the forest is no longer confused and obscure, but quite reassuringly clarified. Its spatial relationship to the desert (still associated quite properly with the *selva* since they are equally valid images of primordial disorientation) is almost prosaically definite in Vergil's explanation: "sappi che se' nel secondo girone . . . e sarai, mentre / che tu verrai nell' orribil sabbione." There are sound psychological reasons for the "guided tour" aspect of the infernal journey.

Almost every detail of the infernal wood nevertheless represents an intensification of the horror of its earlier manifestation, an intensification which is at the same time an explanation, in infernal terms, of the sinister aspects implied on the first encounter. Where Dante had lost his way in getting into the first wood, in the infernal wood there is a complete absence of a way: "nessun sentiero era segnato". The *via* in the first wood is described as "smarrita", but here, with greater intensity, Dante describes himself as "tutto smarrito m'arrestai", so bewildered that he was brought to a complete standstill. Where previously he was menaced but not attacked by wild beasts, here the self-destructive, those who have gone all the way in the direction in which Dante was heading, are chased and torn by hunting dogs, *cagne*, animals under orders carrying out an appointed task. The grotesque merging of man and tree in the infernal forest expresses the ultimate condition of loss of identity threatened in the *selva selvaggia*. The unhappy souls have slid back down the path of emergent consciousness and have become identified with the *silva* (the unconscious) in the form of tree spirits. Such identification permits Dante to associate the horror of their situation with the primitive feelings of horror implied not only in the taboo against harming the trees of the sacred grove, but also in the taboo against disturbance of the dead. The resultant image is thus too deeply intertwined and rooted in ancient and powerful feelings to be considered merely the product of superficial allegorical fancy; it is in the profoundest sense symbolic.

We have already looked at some of the earlier associations of the mountain and its beasts. Let us see how these are developed in the *Inferno*. The general shape of Dante's hell is of course that of an inverted mountain, an appropriate image of the infernal sense of the *dilettoso monte* of the opening canto. We do not, of course, realize how precisely this relationship is worked out until we reach the *Purgatorio* (a place where all images are clarified) and learn that the mountain of spiritual ascent was actually created by the same impact (the fall of Lucifer) that created the Inferno itself. The beasts of the mountain reappear in the form of the composite monster Geryon in the *Inferno*; he is indeed linked specifically to the leopard by the poet's enigmatic revelation that the cord with which Vergil signals to Geryon is one with which Dante had once tried to catch "la lonza alla pelle depinta". The beasts, it is clear, will impede one's ascent, but are quite ready to assist one's journey downwards.

The observant reader will have no difficulty in identifying the stages of similar analyses of the other seminal images of the first canto and it would be unnecessary to trace them all fully here. Some developments are relatively simple, for instance the *lago del cor*, which was so piteously afflicted with fear through the night that Dante spends in the *selva oscura*, reappears in allegorical rather than metaphorical form as the frozen lake in the very heart of the underworld. Others, such as those of the *pianeta* and the *città* reappear in ever more complex and subtle transformations as the journey through the afterworlds reaches its climax. There is one complex cluster of images, however, whose development we must look at more closely since it comprises in a unique manner the three elements which we have been distinguishing as basic in this type of medieval allegory: *locus, potentia animae*—the visionary authority —and the dialogue.

This image is difficult to name, owing to its extraordinary pattern of metamorphoses, but we may term it, *faute de mieux*, the guardian of the river. Its seminal manifestation occurs in what we may call the ante-infernal desert, in the person of Vergil himself. Those elements of his image which later turn out to be seminal are: his abrupt appearance at a time of crisis to assist the poet, his venerable and imposing presence, the description of his voice as *fioco*, hoarse or weak, though his speech has been a *largo fiume*, a great river, and his advice to Dante to take another way, *altro viaggio*, than the one he had embarked on. Vergil's seminal significance is not fully defined, however, until the next canto, when Lucia in enigmatic words draws Beatrice's attention to Dante's plight:

> Non vedi tu la morte che il combatte
> su la fiumana, ove il mar non ha vanto . . . (II.107)

Vergil, spurred on in his turn by Beatrice, thus becomes, in terms of the metaphor, the first of the rescuers who will help Dante in his struggle with death on the torrential river over which the sea has no boast. This river has been interpreted either specifically as, for example, an anticipatory reference to Acheron, or generally as the river of life. Both interpretations are in part correct, but blur the essentially dynamic quality of Dantean symbolism. When the words are first spoken by Lucia, they can have no specific significance; it would be quite gratuitous to anticipate Dante's crossing of Acheron, and indeed at this point of the story the reader can have no imaginative foreknowledge of this event.[12] But neither are we intended to let Lucia's description of the river be reduced to mere commonplace. Her precise but provocatively mysterious description should remain in the back of our minds, since such images have a tendency to develop into elucidatory allegories.

During their next and infernal manifestation in the encounter with Charon, the images of Vergil and the *fiumana*, already associated by the implications noted above, become interconnected almost to the point of fusion. Let us first notice the almost humorously elaborate system of echoings and juxtapositions of words and ideas that the poet sets up between the two encounters, with Vergil and with Charon. The ambiguities appear already in the line where the poet begins his description of Acheron: "vidi gente alla riva d'un gran fiume." The phrase "gran fiume" echoes the "largo fiume" which previously described the quality of Vergil's "parlar" (*speech*), the "riva", the bank of the "acqua perigliosa" where, in terms of the metaphor of lines 22–4 of the first canto, Vergil first found Dante, and the image as a whole echoes Lucia's description of Dante's plight. So far, the connections, though definite, are slight, and would be insignificant without considerable confirmation. This the poet amply provides. The last word, "fiume", of the line we have just analysed is found to rhyme with the phrase "fioco lume", "fioco" being, as we have seen, a striking epithet used of Vergil in the first encounter. The phrase as a whole suggests,

---

[12] Among the editors, P. H. Wicksteed and D. L. Sayers interpret it as the river of human life, Sapegno (following Chimenez), the river of human evil. Singleton, in a subtle analysis ("Allegory", pp. 55*ff*.), connects the river with the metaphorical *pelago* of *Inferno* 1.25. Aldo Vallone's words concerning the obscurities of the references to the *Veltro* in the first canto of the *Inferno* are apposite here: "In essi, come invece di frequente in altri, non c'è la minima allusione a future spiegazioni. Perché? Dante, quando parla oscuro pone sempre una riserva del genere: pazientate, o miei lettori, arriverà il tempo che vi spiegherò ogni cosa! (*Studi su Dante Medievale*, Firenze, 1965, p. 134.)

in its rhyming and its play on sounds, the key word "fiume" itself. In reinforcement of these verbal interconnections, after two more stanzas there occurs a line descriptive of Dante's resolution to ask no more questions before they reached Acheron: "infino al fiume dal parlar mi trassi." Here one is tempted to associate the *fiume* with the *parlar*, and thus pick up an echo of the first description of Vergil as "quella fonte, che spande di parlar sì largo fiume." Nor should we miss the implicit allusion to the fact that it was Vergil himself, as the poet of the *Aeneid*, who was for Dante the primary authority for the existence and character of the *fiume* Acheron—in a sense its creator.

Vergil now having been associated with the *fiume* in a number of ways that all but defy rational analysis, we are ready for the similar but more serious association of Vergil with Charon, his dark or underworld aspect, or dimension. Both promise to guide their charges into darkness and torments, but Vergil commands the abandonment of cowardice where Charon commands abandonment of hope. Both insist that Dante should take another way, "altra via", but where Vergil's advice is quite properly obeyed, Charon, with equal propriety, is sternly overruled.

What may our examination of this strange juxtaposition of personality and situation contribute to our understanding of the poem and Dante's view of the spiritual universe? As we might expect, while certain darker aspects of the imagery and the spiritual situation of the opening have been somewhat elucidated—we may infer that those who refuse Vergil's assistance on the *fiume* are likely to encounter his darker manifestation on Acheron—yet in all the mysterious nature of the pattern of correspondences has been rendered rather more than less mysterious. A horrifying disillusion is as much as we have the right to expect on the river of hell. True elucidation must await a higher spiritual state. Indeed, as soon as our travellers reach purgatory we find the same complex image appearing in clearer and nobler dimensions.

The first manifestation of the return of this complex of imagery is the figure of Cato, the guardian of the purgatorial shores, described as:

> un veglio solo,
> degno di tanta riverenza in vista,
> che più non dee a padre alcun figliuolo.
>
> Lunga la barba e di pel bianco mista . . . (1.31)

In his external appearance he resembles Charon, "un vecchio bianco per antico pelo" (*Inferno* III.83), but in mien he is very much a "Vergil figure", to be reverenced as a father. As with the encounter with Charon, resemblances that we might take to be insignificant are strengthened by complex verbal linkages and parallelism of situation. His first words to Vergil and Dante run:

> Chi siete voi, che contro al cieco fiume
> fuggito avete la prigione eterna?

The phrase *cieco fiume* takes us back to the memory of Acheron, the dark river of those who are spiritually blind. It contains also a distant but unmistakable play on the sound and meaning of *fioco lume* which we found to be similarly central in the description of Acheron; it also embodies a more distant but still significant reminder that the person who started this train of events is Lucia, the healer of spiritual as well as physical weakness of sight. Moreover, the lines repeat Charon's natural but mistaken challenge of Dante's right to enter the kingdom whose approaches he guards.

Once more the reluctance of the guardian is overcome by Vergil's intervention, but here the terse and enigmatic words of power which were sufficient to overcome the hostility of Charon are replaced by a long speech of eloquent persuasion, appropriate, in Vergil's mind at least, to the higher status of the guardian. Nonetheless, Cato can find no better word for such eloquence than "lusinghe", and informs Vergil that the authority of a heavenly lady is sufficient to let them pass. In both cases, therefore, we see that the suspicion of the guardian may be dispelled by a simple reference to the authority sponsoring their journey.

The general effect of these connections is reinforced in *Purgatorio* II.65, where Vergil explains to the newly landed souls that he and Dante have also just arrived on these shores "per altra via che fu sì aspra e forte", echoing both Charon's words on the banks of Acheron (*Inferno* III.91) and his own instructions to Dante in *Inferno* 1.91. Simultaneously the line reflects the description of the terrain at the very opening of the poem: "questa selva selvaggia ed aspra e forte". The fusion here of ideas and phrasing from three striking passages from the opening scenes of the *Inferno* constitutes an important commentary on their earlier significance. We are brought to realize that the seminal images of the rough terrain and the "other way" have developed to include all that Dante and Vergil have experienced in the underworld. We may also understand that the asperity of the journey will now be modified by the fact that it is no longer so "other", alien; Dante and Vergil are now joining the main road to salvation.

We may mention briefly some other connections, hardly necessary for reinforcement—one gets the impression that Dante took a kind of pleasure in the juxtaposition of the two situations. Cato politely and helpfully recommends them to return by a different route from their wash in the ocean—"poscia non sia di qua vostra reddita", in order that they may take an easier route of ascent—a pleasing further variation on the theme "Per altra via . . ." Charon's function as ferryman is separated off in this new constellation of the imagery: while Cato takes the role of guardian, the voyage across the ocean is guided by an angelic pilot who, unlike Charon, needs to make no use of his oar even for movement of the boat. It may be recollected that Charon used his oar for prodding on the more sluggish of his passengers. This aspect of Charon's role is nevertheless not lacking in the *Purgatorio*; Cato sternly urges on the *spiriti lenti* who have delayed to hear Casella's song, and the obedient souls respond like "colombi"; at Acheron they had responded "come augel per suo richamo".

To this point, the development of the images of Vergil and the *fiume*, like that of all the images we have begun to analyse, has remained, though brilliant and suggestive, somewhat enigmatic in its significance. Indeed it is not until we reach the garden of the earthly paradise at the top of the mountain that we can begin to make out the outlines of the total pattern. The first thing we may notice is that the images, which up to this point have been diverging into different implications and ramifications, now begin to show a contrary movement of convergence. This convergence occurs on many different levels of significance. In terms of topography, the mountain top forms a simple and natural image of convergence. While all virtues converge in the garden, there is a particular emphasis on the convergence of man's political and ecclesiastical responsibilities, which were so difficult to reconcile in this age. Where the images themselves are concerned, we see a concentration and convergence of (among many others) the *selva, monte, fiume*, the guide over the water and the guardian of the sacred realm. The *selva* is here, as before, the primary image. It is introduced in two significant phrases: *divina foresta* and *selva antica*. It is indeed original and divine in Dante's scheme; all previous manifestations of the *selva* owe what validity they have to their relationship to this one. Its own relationship to its more corrupt manifestations is hinted at here and there: at one point it is referred to as "all that Eve lost"; again, during the pageant of Holy Church, the evil giant drags the Babylonish beast through the forest to conceal his *puttana* from public gaze. More positively, this is the place the poets dreamed of when they sang the Golden Age. The poet's relationship to the forest is now clarified. In its original manifestation in the ante-inferno it had been menacing and alien. In the wood of the suicides Dante would have lost his way again without Vergil to guide him—and he sees there the fate of those who have ultimately lost their way in the forest: they have become trees themselves, a startling image for the complete absorption of man's soul into the regressive forces that threaten him in the infernal manifestations of the forest. Here in Eden, however, man regains mastery over the forest, just as over himself. Dante will be a *silvano* (forester) here for a little while before ascending to the true heavens; he will enact all that Adam was intended to have enacted.

Turning to other important imagery, we find that while the basic functions of the barrier (and its watery nature) remain unchanged, and thus provide a basis for contrast, the characteristic experience of passing through it has been sharply intensified. Dante passed Acheron in a state of temporary unconsciousness, and narrowly escaped the petrification of permanent unconsciousness in attempting to pass through the gates of Dis, but in the passage of the purgatorial barriers the symbol and the experience become increasingly interfused. Instead of the deadening effect of passing into a lower stage of consciousness, a sense is conveyed of the harsh, agonized exaltation of passing into a higher spiritual state. While there is still a considerable gap between symbol and experience at the entrance gate of purgatory, in that Dante can ascend the three steps without undergoing the full brunt of the spiritual preparation these steps symbolize, on leaving purgatory he has to expose himself entirely to the final purifying fire—that *foco d'amor* (VI.38), which has already been anticipated in Vergil's enigmatic words as fulfilling in a moment all the satisfaction due for an individual's transgressions. Similarly, when he reaches the final river barriers of the Earthly Paradise, there is no longer any method of passing over the waters untouched; Dante has to be thoroughly immersed in them by Matilda, and made to drink from them before he can attain a higher state of spiritual consciousness. Indeed, both Beatrice and Matilda, whose roles in guarding Lethe-Eunoe are quite parallel to the twin functions of challenger and guide performed by Cato and the angel on the antepurgatorial shores, show a more intense seriousness about their duties. Beatrice's challenge is not as formal as that of Cato or the angel at purgatory's gate; but before Dante crosses the river his qualifications are challenged in a cross-examination more searing in its effect than anything in the *Inferno*.

The concentration of imagery that occurs in the Earthly Paradise has, therefore, two aspects. We find the important images in closer proximity and more intimately related than before, but, more important, we find certain images that previously had a relatively formal, institutional, or ritual tone have gained extraordinarily in spiritual intensity.

Of the methods Dante employed in describing a journey to the celestial paradise, his use of landscape imagery in a region traditionally considered by theologians beyond all imagery stands out as exemplary of the successful fusion of earthly and transcendental elements. The depiction of imagery which is irradiated with a greater spiritual intensity than in any previous description is achieved in the *Paradiso* by a method similar to that employed in the last cantos of the *Purgatorio*—the convergence and the further development of the clusters of images already established in the poem. The primary image of convergence in the *Paradiso* is the garden, *orto* or *giardino*, a natural image for expressing the harmonious conjunction of all previous landscape images. These terms for garden are used by Dante only sparsely in the *Commedia* before the *Paradiso*, and each time in a strongly negative sense. Significantly enough, the terrestrial paradise is never described directly as a garden, though its characteristics as well as tradition would suggest this.[13]

<hr />

[13] In *Inferno* XXIX.129, Siena is referred to obliquely as a garden of prodigality where costly spices grow to appease the gluttonous; in *Inferno* XXXIII.119, the Friar Alberigo refers to himself as "quel delle frutte del mal orto", the fruit of the evil garden whose appearance at his dinner table was the signal for a treacherous murder. In *Purgatorio* VI.105 Dante inveighs against the Emperors who have permitted Italy, "il giardin dell'" imperio", to be laid waste.

In Dante's dialogue with Bonaventura concerning the spiritual exploits of Dominic the first use occurs of the new clusters of landscape imagery in the *Paradiso*. A prophetic dream is mentioned concerning the *mirabile frutto* of the spiritual heirs that will proceed from Dominic; he is described as *agricola* in Christ's orchard (*orto*), and finally by a third switch of imagery he is described as the one from whom will flow various streams (*diversi rivi*) for the watering of the orchard.

These loosely associated image-patterns are typical of Dante's use of imagery in dialogue, as opposed to the allegory proper. Dante avoided too consistent an allegory within dialogue: it would have competed dangerously with the reader's imaginative vision of the main allegory. At the same time he prepares the reader for a more sustained development of these images by their seminal employment in a loose cluster of associated metaphors.

The preparatory use of the garden image is reinforced in the twenty-third canto when Dante, dazzled by the vision of the full assembly of heaven, is encouraged by Beatrice to turn his gaze away from her to contemplate the celestial hosts,

> Perchè la faccia mia sì t'innamora,
> che tu non ti rivolgi al bel giardino
> che sotto i raggi di Cristo s'infiora?
>
> Quivi è la Rosa, in che il Verbo divino
> carne si fece. . . .[14]   (XXIII.70–74)

With this encouragement Dante turns his face once more to the vision, but cannot see the garden or the rose, merely, at this point, a "turbe di splendori" (*a throng of splendours*), which he compares to, but does not precisely visualize as, a "prato di fiori" (*a meadow full of flowers*). The metaphor and the vision have not yet become one.

The next stage of development of the image of the garden occurs in the twenty-sixth canto, where Dante, temporarily blinded by the radiance of the vision of St. John, is discoursing with him on the

---

[14] In *Paradiso* XXIII.20–21 Dante has just termed the blessed "frutto Ricolto del girar di queste spere", where the turning of the spheres should probably be identified with the total historical process. See C. S. Lewis's exegesis in *Medieval and Renaissance Literature* (Cambridge, 1966), p. 91, in a paper which treats extensively (rather than structurally) garden and other imagery of the last eleven cantos of the *Paradiso*.

effects of the divine love, which is responsible, Dante says, for having drawn him from the ocean of wicked love (*mar dell' amor torto*) and placed him on the shores (*riva*) of the love that is righteous. In the conclusion of this speech he returns once more to make his own first use of the image of the garden, which has occurred so far only in the utterance of the beings who have been explaining heaven and the nature of blessedness to him.

> Le fronde, onde s'infronda tutto l'orto
> dell' ortolano eterno, am' io cotanto,
> quanto da luï a lor di bene è porto.
>
> (xxvi.64)

The use of the imagery is still metaphorical. Dante cannot yet see the direct vision of the *orto eterno*, but his imagery embodies in miniature the essence of his pilgrimage. Moreover, he has come to recognize his surroundings as a garden—psychologically, as we have seen, the place where the claims of intuition and reason are reconciled. The use of the word *orto* links the realms of the Lord in both heaven and earth, for Dominic has already been termed a worker and an irrigating river in the *orto cattolico*, and Dante is already aware, at least by report if not yet by direct vision, of his proximity to the *bel giardino* of the heavenly hosts. Significantly the conclusion of this speech of Dante's is followed by the restoration of his sight by Beatrice.

The stage is now set for the final vision of heaven, in the thirtieth canto of the *Paradiso*, where all imagery meets in its final point of concentration, in the empyrean of pure light, "il ciel, ch'è pura luce". Here his eyes first become capable of perceiving the archetypal river of light, and the garden which surrounds it:

> E vidi lume in forma di riviera
> fulvido di fulgore, intra due rive
> dipinte di mirabil primavera.
>
> Di tal fiumana uscian faville vive,
> e d'ogni parte si mettean nei fiori. . . . (xxx.61)

But this garden of light is itself only the "shadowy prefaces" of the final image of reality, the disclosure to Dante of the great court of heaven in the form of the *rosa sempiterna*, referred to by St. Bernard as a *giardino*. In these final scenes all the landscape metaphors of the *Paradiso* merge together and transform themselves into the image of the ultimate reality—the stream; the *fiumana*; the guide who, under the prompting of Lucia, makes clear the eyesight and guides into the realm over the river; the garden as the point of concentration representing the harmony of all the previous landscape imagery; and the vision of the single rose, as a final concentration and transcendence, inclusive rather than exclusive, of the garden image itself.

This vast movement from seminal image to allegory, to celestial archetype, which we have been attempting to outline is, while quite typical of medieval allegory in its basic structure, developed far beyond any previous work. Not only is the development of imagery more complex than in any other allegory, but Dante shows a greater awareness of his use of this structural principle. We can detect this in such passages as Matilda's description of the Earthly Paradise as a pledge (*arra*) of eternal peace, or Beatrice's description of the garden of light in the celestial paradise as nothing but shadowy prefaces (*ombriferi prefazii*) of the truth. In the total structural pattern of this imagery nothing is left out: all aspects of the landscape of Dante's first experience of the dark wood and every aspect of hell and purgatory which comment on those seminal phenomena finally play their part in the process of convergence and spiritualization that culminates in the sempiternal rose. What is confused or mysterious in its lower manifestations is inevitably resolved by allegorical analysis into its constituent metaphysical archetypes. Lastly, let us note that while the polarization of images of earthly experience into their ultimate essences is more intense and far-reaching than in any other medieval allegory, correspondingly the tension under which this process of analysis and ultimate fusion is achieved is of an equivalent emotional and spiritual extremity.

DANTE'S DIALOGUES

As Dante pursues his travels through his worlds of vision we soon become aware that the weight of his report is as much on his dialogues with the dead as on simple description of the realms they inhabit. At first the tone and purport of these dialogues appear extraordinarily diverse in comparison with those we have looked at in earlier visions. Most of Dante's dialogues are related to the landscapes the poet and his guide are passing through, but in very varying degrees and manners. Some consist of little more than identification of the *locus* and a relatively straightforward explication of its spiritual significance, usually provided by Vergil in the underworld, and by the local inhabitants in purgatory and paradise. These explications sometimes bring out important implications of the scene before them, as in Vergil's enigmatic aphorism that makes love the right scourge for envy (*Purgatorio* XIII.37–42), or in Piccarda's clarification of her accord with the divine will, even in the outermost and least glorious of the paradisal spheres (*Paradiso* III.64–90).

Frequently, too, the dialogue develops into full-length disquisitions on various topics in which interest has been stimulated by the *locus* in question. Here Anchises's explication of the transmigration of souls would have provided an example (*Aeneid* VI.707ff.) A philosophical discussion of the goddess Fortune arises out of the sight of the punishment of the prodigal and the avaricious who have failed to comprehend her greatness as well as her limitations (*Inferno* VII). The encounter with the sinister red stream gushing out of the wood of the suicides leads to Vergil's half scientific, half allegorical, disquisition on the rivers of hell (*Inferno* XIV). Dante's surprise at the northward movement of the sun in purgatory stimulates a genuinely scientific astronomical explanation of the apparent position of the heavenly bodies in the southern hemisphere (*Purgatorio* V).

This last example is, however, somewhat exceptional in that it expatiates on the geographical significance of the *locus* in a manner unrelated to its spiritual significance. For the most important function of the dialogue in the *Commedia*, as in visionary allegory in general, is the expression of the intellectual aspects of the journey from psychic dislocation to transcendence. The stages of the ascent seem very similar to those we have looked at previously, as for example in Alan's *Complaint of Nature*, though the manner of presentation is very different. In each of these works the dialogue expresses the intellectual aspects of the process by which the evils within the soul are identified, analysed, confronted and purged, and the corresponding virtuous qualities similarly identified in order to be accepted and participated in by the visionary, with the aid of figures representative successively of the operations of nature and of grace.

But to find such similarities in the function of the dialogue in these two works is only to become more aware of the enormous differences in their struture, especially in the relationships of the dialogue to the other elements of the allegory. More than any previous allegorist, Dante has linked his therapeutic dialogue very closely to images of landscape. Typically, it is stimulated by encounters with specific persons and places. In the *Complaint* there is only Lady Nature's sense of rhetorical structure to shape the experiences of vice and virtue to which the reader is exposed. The strife of these contraries is represented in mythological narrative and pageant, as well as in conceptual terms, but the various divisions of the subject do not arise out of a progression of experience as in the *Commedia*. Such "set piece" orations cannot have the immediate impact of discourse stimulated directly by experience. Dante's intricate ordering of the landscapes of the afterworlds provides, in addition, a more complex and subtle type of categorization than in the *Complaint*. While Jean de Hanville and Guillaume de Lorris achieved a closer relationship between *locus* and dialogue than Alan, it is only in the vision of the *Pearl* (a work almost certainly influenced by the *Commedia*) that an equally forceful confrontation with *locus* and *potentia* provides the stimulus for the dialogue, and where the dialogue, in its turn, furnishes a similar intellectual preparation for the revelation of *loci* of a higher spiritual order.

One type of dialogue, uniquely Dantean perhaps, must be termed dramatic rather than intellectual in its mode of contribution to the total effect of the allegory. This dramatic dialogue is frequently associated with the revelation of the earthly antecedents of some soul's spiritual condition. Some such revelations are no more than simple illustrations of the significance of the *locus*, as for example St. Clare's explanation of her presence in the heaven of the inconstant as proceeding from her removal from the conventual life she had vowed. Others powerfully dramatize the state of mind revealed in these confessions of earthly experiences, notably, for instance, Francesca's account of her passion for Paolo, in which her whole style of speech and phrasing betrays a gentle, self-regarding and perhaps self-indulgent softness, as when she replies to Dante's request for her story:

Ma se a conoscer la prima radice
del nostro amor tu hai cotanto affetto,
farò come colui che piange e dice. (*Inferno* v.124–6)

*But if you have such a desire to know the earliest roots of our love, I shall
have to act as one who weeps as she speaks.*

The direct relevance of the psychotherapeutic process appears
to vary from place to place in the *Commedia*. We become intensely
aware of its effects in the dialogues at such moments of crisis as the
poet's first encounters with his spiritual guides Vergil and Beatrice,
at his crossing of the major spiritual frontiers, and during his
explicit participation in the purgations of the mountain. There is
one type of dialogue, however, which sometimes seems to have
little immediate relevance to either the spiritual place in which it
occurs or to the poet's own journey towards salvation. The frequent
outbursts against the wickedness of political and social mores on
earth, while appropriate enough to the tone of the *Inferno*, seem
particularly inappropriate and digressive in the *Paradiso*, where
one would expect the felicity of the blessed to be undisturbed by
such preoccupations; in fact such outbursts are twice explicitly
referred to as digressions, once when Dante's encounter with the
patriotic poet Sordello leads him into a powerful remonstrance
against the failings of the Italy of his own day (*Purgatorio* vi.128),
and again in the *Paradiso* (xxix.127) where Beatrice excuses herself
for the length of her digression on false preachers and pardoners.

Nonetheless, at whatever cost in the relevance of the dialogue to
the *locus* in question, Dante's continuing commentary on earthly
failings succeeds in creating a new view of our own world in the
Commedia; paradoxically we see it for once as the other world, *sub
specie aeternitatis*. At the end of the *Troilus*, Chaucer's hero can
laugh at the pettiness of this world from the "holoughness of the
eighthe spere". Dante in the spheres finds the earth a subject for
tears, not laughter. Such difference in response points to the reason
for the constant use of digression for the creation of a detailed and
sombre picture of mundane existence. Troilus is finished with the
problems of this life; Dante is not. The purpose of the *Commedia*,
as defined in the letter to Can Grande (para. 15), is to remove those
living in a state of misery and to lead them into the state of felicity.
If Dante had ignored the miseries of earthly life in pure contemplation of the state of felicity, he would have failed in this purpose and

indeed in a sense have been guilty himself of a "gran rifiuto". For Dante, the quest for personal salvation does not imply a turning of one's back on the affairs of this world. It could be argued that he thus at times sacrificed the credibility and the artistic coherence of his vision to his moral purpose. To this one might answer that the vision need not and indeed cannot be regarded as an objective account of the realities of the other world, but must be seen, in this respect at least, as subjective—as the vision of an earthly creature on whom the affairs of earth can never cease to press, whether our criterion is to be moral purpose or artistic coherence.[15]

Historically speaking, the appearance of the *potentia* to give stern advice or prophecy concerning matters vital to the political or moral welfare of the state is highly appropriate to the genre (or the psychology) of the visionary experience. Earlier visions in the western tradition—those of Mesopotamia, Egypt and Israel—had scarcely been concerned with any other topics, and the visionary appearance of Cicero's Scipio and Vergil's Anchises in similar roles would have been familiar to Dante. It is therefore not surprising that from a formal as well as a moral point of view the syncretism of the *Commedia* should have included powerful, outspoken and authoritative comment on the political and moral crises of the period.

THE FIGURE OF BEATRICE

The role of Beatrice as the major *potentia* of the *Comedy* has already been touched upon earlier in this chapter, in so far as her manifestations form part of the development of the major images from the seminal stage to the higher dimensions of their reality. In this regard she is the celestial manifestation of the image we earlier termed "the guide over the dark river", whose seminal form appeared in the instructions of Lucia to Beatrice to assist Dante in his desperate struggle on the river "over which the sea has no

[15] Another important example of this category is the dialogue between Forese and Dante (*Purgatorio* XIII) in which not only Forese's location in the circle of the repentant gluttonous is explained, but also something of Dante's own similar way of living, which had necessitated his rescue by Vergil and his journey through the realms of the afterworld.

vantage".[16] But to gauge something of her imaginative impact on a medieval audience, we also need to understand her archetypal, symbolic dimensions.

Her first appearance in the works of Dante, in the opening of the *Vita Nuova*, gives us an indication of the ambiguities which underlie the many dimensions of the imagination in which she functions. Like other medieval works treating of love and philosophy, the *Vita* opens with the mysterious appearance of an awe-inspiring female figure,

> alli miei occhi apparve . . . la gloriosa donna
> della mia mente, la quali fu chiamata da molti
> Beatrice, i quali non sapeano che si chiamare.

Her introduction seems intentionally ambiguous. If we consider her as existing primarily in external reality, we may understand that those who called her Beatrice did not realize the inner significance of her name as "bestower of blessing", whereas when we consider her existence as primarily internal and allegorical ("la gloriosa donna della mia mente" in the deeper sense), we may understand that many knew her in the spiritual life who were unaware of her name on earth. In our terms, many who knew her in everyday life did not understand that she was a manifestation of the *potentia*, whereas many who were aware of the existence of this *potentia* did not realize that it had manifested itself in Beatrice.

Let us first attempt to determine the general characteristics of this new manifestation of the *potentia* and then examine the extraordinary circumstance of a *potentia* manifesting itself in a living person. In the opening of the *Vita Nuova* it is left ambiguous whether the lady is to be thought of as the object of courtly love or of spiritual veneration; in terms of the *Roman de la Rose*, whether Beatrice is to be associated with the Rosebud or the Lady Reason. Dante maintains these ambiguities throughout the *Vita* and indeed the *Commedia* itself; it is hardly too much to say that they form the basis of his statement about the relationship of earthly and heavenly love.

The appearance of Beatrice produces extreme perturbation of spirit in the youthful Dante, and from that moment he acknowledges the lordship of Love over his soul. The situation seems very

[16] See above pp. 125–6.

similar to that in the *roser* when the dreamer falls in love, but the perturbation is also parallel to the stupefaction ("obstipui") of Boethius at first seeing *Philosophia*, or the confusion of Alan at the sight of *Natura*. Finally we learn that "la sua immagine . . . era di si nobile virtù, che nulla volta sofferse, che Amore mi reggesse senza il fedele consiglio della ragione . . ." Such is the "nobile virtù" of this lady that Reason is reconciled to Dante's love for her, the resulting association of Love and Reason foreshadowing that of Beatrice and Vergil in the *Commedia*.

The same pattern of ambiguity is present when the mature Dante succeeds at last in finding Beatrice again in the Paradise Garden on Mount Purgatory. Here she is in one sense the venerable lady, corresponding to *Natura* or the Madonna, in her natural setting; in another she is the beloved, the Rose of the garden, who agrees to pardon the lover after he has merited most severe treatment from the lady's "daunger"; in a third, she is Jean's Resoun as she might have reproached the wilful Amant, offering herself as his "amie de si haut lignage".[17]

Dante is not merely parodying the conventions of courtly love to express religious ideas with more force and immediacy, as was the case with Jean. Rather he is suggesting a resolution of the problems of courtly love by its absorption into the scheme of divine love and mercy, that is, so far as its ethos and patterns of behaviour may be redeemed. It is not surprising that this redemption of earthly love should find its fullest expression in his Paradise Garden, which is also in other senses his place of redemption of what is worthiest in earthly life.

The figure of Beatrice, however, has a significance in the development of the visionary *potentia* that goes beyond the aspects we have been describing. Previously, the *potentia* had been based on the figure of a god or goddess, or the closely related figure of the allegorical abstraction. Now it begins to manifest itself in the form of a person encountered in the poet's everyday experience, or in a figure of history, especially sacred history. The shift in emphasis in the character of the *potentia* may be appropriately illustrated by reference to the *Pastor of Hermas*, since this early Christian

[17] An important monograph by Luigi Alfonsi has shown the considerable extent to which Dante echoes the relationship of Boethius and Lady Philosophy in his depiction of the relationship of the poet and Vergil, and especially the poet and Beatrice, in the *Commedia* (*Dante e la "Consolatio Philosophiae" di Boezio*, Como, 1944, pp. 513–21).

allegory opens in a manner that seems directly to anticipate the manifestation of Beatrice in the *Vita Nuova* and the *Commedia*.

The narrator first relates the innocent-seeming infatuation he once felt for the Lady Rosa, whose slave he had been in youth and whom he had later desired as a wife after once seeing her bathing in the Tiber. Wandering into the countryside he is carried away by the spirit and finds himself in an impassable wilderness. Crossing a torrential river he comes to a plain where:

As I prayed, the heavens were opened, and I saw the woman whom I had desired saluting me from the sky, and saying "Hail Hermas!"And looking up to her I said, "Lady, what doest thou here?" And she answered me, "I have been taken up here to accuse you of your sins before the Lord."[18]

In the dialogue that follows between the lady and Hermas, she reproves him for his sins and advises him to pray for forgiveness. The whole incident comprises no more than the first chapter of the first book of Hermas. The remaining twenty-four chapters consist of dialogues with a *domina* on the subject of sin and redemption, but instead of permitting Roda to continue in her function (which is to anticipate Beatrice), in the very next chapter the author replaces her by the allegorical figure of the *Mater Ecclesia*. And in the second and third books the "shepherd" himself, the angel of repentance, is responsible for the instruction of Hermas. We have here a clear case of an early allegorist abandoning a well-established human figure as the medium of allegorical instruction, and almost gratuitously substituting an allegorical figure.

Strikingly enough, we have a post-Dantean allegory in which the pattern of the *Shepherd* is completely reversed—Petrarch's *Secretum*. In this work the dreamer, feeling the desperate nature of his spiritual state, is first visited by the allegorical figure, the Lady *Veritas*, who, however, does not herself conduct the long moral dialogue with the poet to help him to a better state of mind. Instead she brings her servant Augustine to perform the function assigned in earlier allegories to a Lady Philosophy or a Lady Nature. It may of course be argued that the Lady Truth appears in acknowledgment of the poet's debt to Boethius, which in this allegory is clearly

---

[18] *The Pastor of Hermas* translated by F. Crombie, I.1, in *The Ante-Nicene Fathers* (Buffalo, N.Y., 1885) II, p. 9.

very strong, but that she is replaced in favour of Augustine in acknowledgment of the debt to Dante, since Petrarch's Augustine has a relationship to *Veritas* analogous to Vergil's relationship to Beatrice. But I believe that there is more to the switch than this, that we are at this point in an age which genuinely felt itself more comfortable with a living figure rather than an allegorical abstraction for the *potentia* of its spiritual dialogues.

What is the evidence of a general change of taste, perhaps even a change in the manner of perception? From the thirteenth century onwards, allegorists increasingly base their stories around the encounter of the narrator with a single specific individual rather than with a personified abstraction. Already in the *Romance of the Rose* it is possible to see the lineaments of the lady behind the abstract figures and concrete symbols that represent various aspects of her effect on the dreamer.[19] Nonetheless, the great step towards modern conceptions was clearly Dante's figure of Beatrice, after which allegories based on concrete personalities became frequent. In England one thinks of the *Pearl*, or Lydgate's *Temple of Glas*, of James's *Kingis Quair*, and of Dunbar's *The Thrissil and the Rois* and *Goldyn Targe*. But the older tradition of abstraction-based allegory did not by any means die out so soon. Gawain Douglas's *King Hart* is as abstract as Prudentius's *Psychomachia*, as are indeed almost all the morality plays until the *Respublica* and other political moralities of the sixteenth century.[20] Chaucer's *Hous of Fame* and *Parlement of Foules* are so esoteric (or perhaps so cautious) that in spite of extensive modern research, we cannot yet definitely say whether these works refer to specific predicaments of individuals or only to the problems of men and women in general.[21]

By and large we may say that the centuries that followed the

[19] Cf. Lewis, *The Allegory of Love*, pp. 118ff. Muscatine has shown that the portrait of the "lady" of the narrator's affections owes much to the romance tradition ("The Emergence of Psychological Allegory in Old French Romance", *PMLA*, December 1953).

[20] Later in the century the morality seems no longer to be able to stand on its own feet as allegory, and as Tucker Brooke says in *A Literary History of England* (edited by A. C. Baugh, New York, 1948, p. 365), "a stiffening for the wilted allegory is found by introducing stories from the Bible, classical literature, or even medieval fiction."

[21] F. N. Robinson summarizes his account of the discussion of contemporary allusions in the *Parlement*: ". . . a personal application of the poem, though undeniably possible, still seems to be by no means necessary" (*The Complete Works of Geoffrey Chaucer*, Cambridge, Mass., 1957, p. 791).

Commedia saw the maintenance of the balance of abstract, symbolical and circumstantial features that first clearly appeared in the allegorical figure of Beatrice, and that has made her so difficult for modern critics to interpret. In the Renaissance we find Spenser basing allegorical figures on characters out of literary as much as personal experience; while in the masque, as Miss Tuve has shown us, the allegorical or mythological figures represented were frequently assumed as roles by those in whom the qualities symbolized manifested themselves in real life (as if Gloriana should have been acted by Queen Elizabeth in a dramatic version of the *Faerie Queene*).[22]

So far, we have been attempting to answer "how" questions about the figure of Beatrice: how it resembles and how it differs from earlier allegorical figures, as a basis for understanding its true significance and uniqueness. There remains a final and almost unanswerable "why" question: why does the creation of such a figure as Beatrice, half symbolic and half actual, seem so inevitable in this period and so impossible in earlier periods? The answer undoubtedly lies in processes more general than any purely literary development, and rather in the development of the medieval consciousness as a whole. The answer would have to be sought not only in literature but in art, philosophy, and theology. One can instance, as symptoms of the process, the growing nominalism of the fourteenth century—the insistence that reality proceeds primarily from the object rather than from the concept; the artist's growing concern with perspective, as giving the objects within his vision a primary relationship to each other within terrestrial space, a relationship which assumes the validity of the object as a thing in itself rather than a secondary and individual manifestation of a system of abstractions whose superior reality depends eventually on the superior reality of God himself.

[22] Rosemond Tuve, *Images and Themes in Five Poems by Milton* (Cambridge, Mass., 1967), pp. 116–21.

8

Pearl

THE "ERBER GRENE"

THE *Pearl*, as we should now expect of a visionary medieval allegory, opens with the poet in a state of deep mental distress. After some six lines devoted to a description of the perfections of a certain pearl of peerless qualities, we are startled by his anguished cry:

> Allas! I leste hyr in on erbere;
> Þurȝ gresse to grounde hit fro me yot.   (9–10)

The *erber* where the pearl was lost becomes a place of mourning for the poet, but the anguish of his loss is strangely harmonized and transformed by the beauties of the garden.[1] As he mourns the pearl that once brought him so much joy, he hears a mysterious sweet singing in the still hours of his sadness. The *erber* blooms in the sunlight with a luxuriance of flowers and spices that springs from the richness of the soil in which the pearl lies rotting, a theme of transformation echoed in images of harvest, of the living grass growing from the dying seed.

Finally the poet's gaze turns inward to the *psychomachia*, to identify the powers at war within his anguished soul:

> Bifore þat spot my honde I spenned;
> For care ful colde þat to me caȝt
> A deuely dele in my hert denned.
> Þaȝ Resoun sette myseluen saȝt
> I playned my perle þat þer watȝ spenned

---

[1] An account of the type of garden implied by the term *erber* will be found in C. A. Luttrell's "*Pearl*, Symbolism in a Garden Setting", in *Sir Gawain and Pearl, Critical Essays* edited by Robert J. Blanch (Indiana, 1966), pp. 6o*ff*., referred to hereafter as Blanch.

Wyth fyrce skylleʒ þat faste faʒt;
þaʒ Kynde of Kryst me comfort kenned,
My wreched wylle in wo ay wraʒte. (49–56)

Though Reason attempts to calm him and Nature acquaints him
with the comfort of Christ, his fierce questionings and wretched
wilfulness permit him no peace. It may first seem mysterious that
it is Nature who shows the poet the comfort of Christ.[2] Should
there not be here a theological, supernatural comfort especially for
one suffering from anguish and bereavement? Should we not be
thinking primarily of Christ of the Resurrection, overcoming death?
Seemingly so, and at a first reading of the poem the phrase might
remain enigmatic. But in fact we have already been shown how
Nature manifests the comfort of Christ, primarily in the symbolisms of harvest and the resurrection of the seed, identifications for
which there is the scriptural source in *John* XII.24. Moreover,
beyond this instance, it will be found that all the specific details of
the world of nature described in the opening stanzas of the poem
later reveal themselves to be seminal images, which will be transformed into the constituents of the world of glory that the dreamer
encounters in his vision of consolation.

But before we turn to the vision itself, let us take note of one
final detail from these opening stanzas, the striking expression the
poet uses for his falling asleep:

I slode vpon a slepyng-slaʒte (59)

The word "slaʒte" has been connected with the Old English
"slaeht", meaning "sudden onset" or "blow". But such an interpretation would do a double injustice to a poet who never employs
a word in vain. One cannot slide (*slode*) into "a sudden blow or
onset". In the context "Slaʒte" must indicate "death by slaying",
and indeed, as we shall eventually see, with reference to one particular death by slaying. But for the moment, we may translate the
line very literally as "I slid into a sleeping-slaying", and from this

[2] Quotations from the *Pearl* from E. V. Gordon's edition (Oxford,
1953). In this instance I have altered Gordon's punctuation (developing
a suggestion made to me by A. K. Hieatt) to bring out the parallelism—
inescapable I believe in this period—between *Resoun* and *Kynde* (Nature).
The present interpretation also permits line 55 to be translated literally,
obviating the need to supply a definite article before *Kynde*.

we may get our first hint of the truth that the death which precedes resurrection ("vch gresse mot grow of grayneʒ dede") applies not only to everything of Nature that the poet has seen in the *erber*, but also, in some manner, to the poet himself.

THE ARTIFICE OF ETERNITY

The five opening stanzas of the poem form a remarkable prelude to the vision proper. Certainly all allegories we have so far examined have displayed the same structural feature—a preliminary description of the poet's disturbed mental state, within which occur metaphors or seminal images that develop into central features or themes of the main allegorical action, the vision itself. But in previous allegories the disturbed state of mind of the poet seems to blot out all details of the poet's external life. The preliminary or seminal images in the *Pearl* are more numerous than in other allegories, are uniquely taken from the poet's external, waking experience, and also, as I hope to demonstrate, are linked to the main action of the work by a series of subtly interconnected transformations, unparalleled in complexity outside the *Commedia*. Moreover, not only are the main symbols of the vision anticipated in this prelude, but the very mode of transformation, as Nature foreshadows in the death and rebirth of the seed the spiritual resurrection of the life to come.

The pearl itself is, as might be expected, the most developed of these symbols, and in addition constitutes a principle of unification which harmonizes the disparate symbols into a set of interrelated meanings. In the preliminary phase of the poem, though we are not led to make any specific interpretations of the pearl, the intensity and gravity of the poet's grief, the solemn tones in which he describes the sweet songs of consolation and the beautiful garden in which his loss occurred, lead us to expect a revelation of a proportionately profound significance in the pearl's loss.

Exhausted by his anguish, the poet falls into a dream of a wonderful country, a land where crystal cliffs encompass a forest of overwhelming beauty. In this dazzling landscape we find all the features of the *erber grene* raised to a state of visionary transformation. Most immediately striking is the fact that the forest is gravelled with precious pearls:

> þe grauayl þat on grounde con grynde
> Wern precious perleȝ of Oryente: (81-2)

But to the dreamer these pearls are no more than gravel grinding under his feet; he does not stoop down and fill his pockets—a confirmation of our impression that the original pearl he lost was more than a physical object. Moreover, the contrast between his one pearl, now lost apparently beyond recovery among the grasses of the garden, and the prodigal profusion of pearls in this land of vision provides a suggestion, later to be justified in the event, that his loss is to receive infinite recompense in this land.

In a similar manner, the other symbols of the *erber* reappear in forms that supersede their earlier manifestations. Where the plants of the arbor and the corn in the fields have been described as subject to death and birth—the cycles of mortal life, the trees of the forest rustle and gleam as if they were made of silver, which we can confidently interpret, in the light of what we learn later, as a symbol of immortality. The bird song in the forest excels all earthly music and is untouched by the sadness associated with the mysterious song of consolation of the opening stanzas. The sun, which shone so brightly on the flowers of the *erber*, is now outshone by the brightness of the pearls on the forest floor.

But while the imagery of the *erber* has undergone radical transformation, we are still ignorant of the precise sense in which such transformation should be interpreted. Jewelled landscapes cannot be considered to have an unvarying archetypal significance, since, for example, the jewelled Garden of the Gods in the *Gilgamesh* epic undoubtedly belongs to an eternal or transcendent world, but it is a place of bitter disappointment to the hero in his search for eternal life. The Bowre of Blisse in the second book of the *Faerie Queene* is a garden where the beauties of nature are supplemented by imitative art work in precious metals, but we can hardly interpret the Bowre as representing anything but a dangerous illusion of joy and harmony, a deceptive imitation of transcendence. The symbolism here, as always, has to be interpreted in the light of the context. The nature of the woodland landscape in the *Pearl* is conveyed to us through illustrative imagery rather than direct interpretation. As often in allegorical landscape, the barriers provide good indications. The river barrier which the dreamer encounters after penetrating some distance into the wood is as subtle in its imagery and implications as any we have seen. In the river, the poet tells us, the pebbles were jewels that glowed as if seen through glass, just as the stars shine on a winter night while mortal men sleep.

> In þe founce þer stonden stoneȝ stepe,
> As glente þurȝ glas þat glowed and glyȝt,
> As stremande sterneȝ, quen stroþe men slepe,
> Staren in welkyn in wynter nyȝt.
>
> (113–16)

Here the jewels of the garden have, in simile, been transformed into stars, and the river into glass. But in this visionary land the similes reveal more truth than the dreamer consciously apprehends. For, as it will later appear, the river barrier, insubstantial as it first seems to the dreamer, is the ultimate barrier between time and eternity, between the highest visionary experience possible in this world, and the perfectly illumined existence of the transcendent world. So, in looking into the river, the dreamer is looking at the barrier separating him from that realm, and is therefore looking "through a glass darkly". He sees the stars, the very outskirts and border-lands of Heaven, not subject to Fortune "under the moon", but controlled by planetary spirits perfectly obedient to the will of God.[3] But the *stroþe men* (perhaps "earthy" or even "swamp" men) being spiritually asleep, as the simile implies, do not see the stars as the frontiers of eternity.

The beauty of the landscape was such, the dreamer tells us, that his anguish quite disappeared (121–4). And yet, it seems he has hardly arrived at a state of enlightenment. He is still under the domination of "Fortune" whom he considers responsible for his present happiness in the woodland "frith", as well as, it is implied, his former sorrow in the *erber* (98, 129–32). He has no understanding of the true nature of the river he has encountered (137–44), or, as it will appear, of the deeper significance of the landscape itself. The poet's awareness of his ignorance, as well as his enlightenment, await the next phase of the poem—the dialogue with the pearl maiden herself.

[3] See C. S. Lewis, *The Discarded Image* (Cambridge, 1964), pp. 97ff.

In the pearl maiden the processes of the allegory find a rational voice. The dreamer's misunderstandings of his situation prompt her to elucidate the manner in which the symbols of his own world have undergone transformation. With naive passion he first enquires of the maiden:

> What wyrde hatȝ hyder my ieul vayned,
> And don me in þys del and gret daunger? (249–50)

He implies that the whole transcendent realm is still under the dominion of fate, *wyrd*, which we may associate with the "Fortune" he believes has brought him here. But the maiden does not immediately correct his mistake about the nature of *wyrd*; first she has to clarify the nature of the subordinate transformations:

> Sir, ȝe haf your tale mysetente,
> To say your perle is al awaye,
> þat is in cofer so comly clente
> As in þis gardyn gracios gaye, . . . (257–60)

The *cofer* (ambiguously treasure chest or coffin—both meanings were common in the period) has been transformed into the garden by a kind of effortless natural magic hinging on the adverb *as*. The identification of these very disparate images—the claustrophobic, brutally physical coffin of the body's last resting place, and the joyous paradise garden prepared for the souls of the innocent—is the first of a series of shocks that should jolt our earthbound preconceptions into the beginning of an understanding of the realities of the pearl maiden's transcendent world, its "strengþe of ioye," its infinite richness of dimension.

In the next stanza the imagery of resurrection is further developed:

> For þat þou lesteȝ watȝ bot a rose
> þat flowred and fayled as Kynde hyt gef.
> Now, þurȝ Kynde, of þe kyste þat hyt con close
> To a perle of prys hit is put in pref.[4] (269–73)

---

[4] *Cf. Romaunt of the Rose* 1680–4, and above. p. 102. *Cf.* also Wendel Johnson in "The Imagery and Diction of *The Pearl:* Toward an Interpretation" *English Literary History* 20 (September 1953), pp. 170–71.

The rose that flowers and fails has become a pearl of price. This important transformation gives us the key to the symbolism of the jewelled landscape. The transient flowers of the *erber* have become the eternal jewels of the dream landscape.

Once more the pearl is revealed as the dominant symbol. The maiden does not explain much about the cause of this transformation, for the dreamer, being still under the influence of his belief in Fortune, is not ready for this. The transformation is thus ascribed to a vague notion of the "nature of the chest" or, if we punctuate boldly as in the above editing of the text, Nature herself.

But, once this is explained, the maiden is ready to say more about *wyrd*, the fate that stands behind the transformation:

> And þou hatჳ called þy wyrde a þef,
> Þat oჳt of noჳt hatჳ mad þe cler;
> Þou blameჳ þe bote of þy meschef,
> Þou art no kynde jueler. (273–6)

By exploiting a subtle and significant ambiguity in the popular conception of *wyrd*, the maiden demonstrates that the Fate which the dreamer has called a thief of the pearl has in fact created for him something out of nothing, an eternal pearl out of a fading rose. Furthermore the phrasing suggests a far profounder conception of fate. "þat oჳt of noჳt hatჳ mad þe cler" contains a hint of a creating power,[5] "þe bote of þe meschef" of a redeeming power. The symbolic transformations of this interchange show the conversion of the idea of fate—God's operations in the universe seen by the untutored, uncomprehending, mortal eye—to the idea of providence—God's operations as seen through the eyes of perfect comprehension, from the "other side of the stream". The entire process may be represented through the transformation of symbols rather than through philosophical dialogue; the more philosophically minded of his audience would already be acquainted with the visionary dialogue in which Boethius is converted to the larger view of *Fortuna*, *Fatum* and *Providentia* by the Lady Philosophy in the second and fourth books of the *Consolation*.

As the dialogue continues, we see the conflict of the opening stanzas between *Resoun* and the "fyrce skylles" acted out and resolved. Other symbolisms receive heightening and amplification at the same time. The harvest motif appears again, but now in the deve-

[5] See A. L. Kellogg's suggestion in *Traditio* XII, pp. 406–7.

loped form of the parable of the vineyard, emphasising no longer the temporal phenomena of death and birth, but the courtesy of heavenly rewards. The dialogue culminates in the maiden's explanation of the significance of the pearl upon her breast; it is at once the pearl of great price for which the jeweller gave all his goods, and the gift of the Lamb in "token of pes". Here it is clear that the maiden does not stand allegorically for the kingdom: the pearl is her chief decoration but, although maiden and jewel are both pearls, they are kept separate. The relationship seems more sacramental than allegorical. The pearl maiden is now "pearl" in that she is not so much an allegory of the kingdom as one of its members, a participant in its essential reality.

The passage also deepens the "jeweller" aspect of the dreamer's role. Previously, as this description appeared in the dialogue, it might have been taken as a fanciful elaboration of the fact that the dreamer in some sense owns the pearl maiden in his role of father. But now the potential of the allegory of dreamer as jeweller is revealed; he is called upon to "sell everything he has" to obtain the pearl of great price, the kingdom.

The dialogue is finally subsumed into vision once more, but one suited to the greater depth and clarity of understanding the dreamer has attained—the vision of the city. In this last phase of the vision, we experience a final transformation of its symbols. Once more the key symbolism is that of the pearl, which, as we realize with some shock of recognition, is the jewel in the *Apocalypse* chosen to form the gates of the heavenly city, where other precious stones are described as forming the walls. It is difficult to avoid the conclusion that the poet has read an allegorical interpretation into the Biblical text here, based on the device developed in the *Romance of the Rose* of contrasting wall and gate symbolisms. It will be recollected that the qualities depicted on the walls of the Park of Lord Mirth were those not admitted inside. To enter, one had to pass by the portress, *Oiseuse*, Leisure.[6] Similarly, in this vision, to pass through the gate of pearl, it is implied, one must have the qualities of childlike innocence that are the keys to the kingdom. Such an interpretation is reinforced by the emphasis in the description of the pearl maiden that she wears pearls and no other gems (206, 219). Within the city, also, neither the Lamb nor the procession of virgins is mentioned as wearing any other jewel. The

[6] *Romaunt*, 132–612.

description of the gates of the City in the *Apocalypse* would therefore be understood, at least in the adaptation in this poem, as
allegorizing the doctrine that "Þe innocent is ay saf by ryʒt." On
the other hand, the virtues symbolized by other stones are, of
course, not entirely excluded by the city—just the opposite in fact.
"Þe woneʒ wdythinne enurned ware Wyth alle kynneʒ perré þat
moʒt repayre." The allegory thus emphasizes the supremacy of the
pearl among stones as the virtue of innocence among virtues. In
this respect the allegorical technique is parallel to and perhaps a
development of that of the *Romance of the Rose*, though not identical to it.

Within the city we find various other seminal images brought
to their final stage of development: the mysterious song of the
opening stanzas now reveals its origin in the song of the blessed:

> Al songe to loue þat gay juelle,
> Þe steuen moʒt stryke þurʒ þe vrþe to helle
> Þat þe Vertues of heuen of joye endyte. (1124–6)

The motif of the outshining of the sun also reaches its final form in
the fantastic fusion of imagery in lines 1045–6:

> Of sunne ne mone had þay no nede;
> Þe self God watʒ her lombe-lyʒt.

The mysterious phrase "slepyng slaʒte", as used to describe
the dreamer falling asleep at the beginning of the poem, undergoes
similar elucidatory transformations: first in the line descriptive of
the crucifixion, "As a schep to the slaʒt þer lad watʒ he", (801) and
then in the final triumphant vision of the wounded Lamb. The
development of the imagery explicates and opens new dimensions
of the use of *slaʒte*. On the semantic level it explains the use of a
word denoting slaughter (or sacrifice) of animals in its harsh and
disturbing initial occurrence in "slepyng-slaʒte".[7] This semantic
connection confirms the participatory parallelism between Christ's
death and resurrection on the one hand and the dreamer's deadly
sleep and spiritual reawakening on the other.

In the final stanza group the thematic phrase, "prynceʒ paye",

[7] See *OED slay* (II, 9) for other examples of the sense, active in this
period, of "To kill (a domestic animal . . .), especially for food or as a
sacrifice. . . ."

elucidates the seminal image of the first line of the poem, "Perle plesaunte to prynces paye". We can now recognize that the manner in which the pearl maiden and the virtues associated with the pearl are pleasant to the "prince" has been one of the main themes of the poem, demonstrated primarily in the heavenly marriage of the pearl maiden to the Lamb, and the Lamb's love of innocence.

The revelation of the character of the prince completes the pattern of development of symbols so far as the dreamer's experience is concerned, but one task remains—to express in terms of the symbolic pattern the reader's or auditor's participation, sought in all serious medieval poetry, in the spiritual benefits of the experience presented. Such participation, the significance of which will be discussed more fully below, is expressed in the closing lines of the prayer, which contain the poet's final resignation of the pearl to God and a prayer for the salvation of both poet and readers:

> And syþen to God I hit bytaȝte
> In Kristeȝ dere blessyng and myn,
> Þat in þe forme of bred and wyn
> Þe preste vus scheweȝ vch a daye.
> He gef vus to be his homly hyne
> Ande precious perleȝ vnto his pay.   (1207–12)

In the prayer Christ is presented to the reader "in þe forme of bred and wyn"—the eucharistic transformation of the earthly symbol to the heavenly reality. This, the most powerful and general of the symbols of transformation within the Christian church, thus represents the type of which the pearl and its associated symbols are but subtypes. Similarly, in the *Gawain* poem in the same manuscript, the green girdle, Gawain's symbol of humility, is juxtaposed in the final prayer against Christ's Crown of Thorns, a primary Christian symbol of humility. But the bread and wine of the eucharist not only symbolize transformation; they also constitute the primary symbols of Christian participation, since it is by participating in the eucharistic feast that "vch a Krysten sawle" enacts what makes him "A longande lym to þe Mayster of myste" (462). Thus the "pearl", like Gawain's girdle, is a symbol directed towards a relatively private and limited event, while the "bred and wyn", and the corresponding Crown of Thorns, turn the more private symbols outward, as it were, and express their relationship to the general situation of Christian man.

This outward movement of symbolic patterns prepares the reader for the final development of the pearl symbolism in the last lines of the poem—the prayer that all may become "precious perleȝ vnto his pay"—where the pearl is transformed from a private, though imaginatively participated symbol, to a general symbol of participation. The reader too must be gathered into this artifice of eternity.

The pattern of transformation thus revealed constitutes an analysis and exploration of earthly symbols and a development of them into an expression of the nature of transcendence. The poem is structured through an extremely complex pattern of transformations at different levels of reality, in which the symbols depend for their efficacy on their imaginative recreation of motifs familiar to the audience not only in previous visionary poetry but in the eternal dreams of the human spirit.

THE PEARL MAIDEN

In interpreting the poem today, the first problem the critic is called upon to decide is whether the "pearl" is primarily a who or a what, or, in other words, whether the poem is an allegory or an elegy. The status of the pearl maiden is scarcely less disputed than that of Dante's Beatrice, and the dispute develops on very much the same lines. Are we to see the maiden as the poet's dead daughter, or is she merely an allegory of some theological virtue that the poet is or ought to be seeking? I believe that the question has often been formulated by modern critics in a manner alien to medieval ways of thought. As in the case of Beatrice, the pearl maiden is interpretable, without any strain on the text, as both a person about whom the poet has the deepest of personal feelings, and also as an embodiment of certain abstract qualities.[8] Generally speaking, the allegorist's aim is to include the maximum number of interpretations compatible and relevant to his main intention, an intention

[8] For this debate see Rene Wellek's "The *Pearl*; an interpretation of the Middle English poem", in Blanch, pp. 10–20, and Stanton Hoffman's "The *Pearl*: Notes for an Interpretation", *Modern Philology* 58 (November 1960), pp. 73–80.

which (as in the case of most serious poetry) can be described but
not defined by prose analysis. If the medieval poet wants to exclude
certain interpretations, he has the liberty of giving a character an
unambiguously allegorical name, Reason, Nature, Nous, or whatever; or, if he wants to emphasize his rejection of certain interpretations, he may use the common allegorical device of the topos of
rejection. The technique of using allegory for disguising meaning
is a later and somewhat decadent development, arising mainly from
misinterpretation of complex allegory as deliberately obscure.

When, however, we turn to the question of whether any exclusively allegorical interpretation is strictly sustainable in the light of
the text, we find that any identification of the pearl maiden with an
allegorical entity is likely to break down when one attempts to
harmonize it with either of two crucial passages in the poem. The
first is the passage where the dreamer says to the pearl maiden that
she

> . . . lyfed not two ȝer in oure þede;
> þow cowþeȝ neuer God nauþer plese ne pray,
> Ne neuer nawþer Pater ne Crede;
> And quen mad on þe fyrst day! (483–6)

At the conclusion of the poem, the dreamer emphasizes his final
acceptance of the loss of the pearl, and her glorification in the New
Jerusalem, in the lines:

> Ouer þis hyul þis lote I laȝte,
> For pyty of my perle enclynin,
> And syþen to God I hit bytaȝte
> In Krysteȝ derc blessyng and myn, . . . (1205–8)

It is difficult to think of any allegorical abstraction which could be
meaningfully made from these remarks, although they are entirely
appropriate to the dreamer's feelings about his dead daughter.

And yet, of course, it is by no means adequate to consider the
pearl maiden as no more than the poet's daughter, *simpliciter*. For,
like all other aspects of temporal reality which find a place in the
main action of the poem, she is shown as transformed and glorified.
In fact, the convincing representation of the maiden as glorified is
the poet's chief imaginative achievement in the poem. She has to
be represented as more impressive than anything we are likely to

meet in this life, and yet at the same time as something in the deepest sense expected, almost inevitable. She has to give the reader the feeling "Yes, I knew all the time it would be like this", although he has never before had such an experience in his conscious life.

The poet's answer to this problem seems at once brilliant, original and inevitable. On the one hand the maiden partakes of the nature of the *potentia animae*, the mistress of dialogue, such as Boethius's Lady Philosophy, or Alan's Lady Nature, particularly in respect of her stern regard for ultimate truth. On the other hand, like Beatrice, she has specifically human dimensions, as the child of the dreamer, which are also susceptible to symbolic interpretation. The symbolism of the child in the *Pearl* has two aspects, which in accordance with our scheme of definitions we may term the *imago* and the archetype. The *imago* we can explain in terms of the Biblical tradition upon which the poet was explicitly drawing. We may note first that the parable of the vineyard is retold at length to bring out the point that the principle of "the first shall be last and the last first" applies very specifically to innocent children, a point that is strengthened later by direct reference to the Dominical utterance:

> . . . hys ryche no wyȝ myȝt wynne
> Bot he com þyder ryȝt as a chylde,
> Oþer elleȝ neuermore com þerinne. (722–4)

In this respect we may say that the *Pearl* develops and fulfils these earlier New Testament intuitions concerning the symbolic significance of the child in much the same way as the gospels amplify and develop Isaiah's original cryptic prophecy of the Kingdom: "And a little child shall lead them."

But we also find a quite unusual problem of interpretation in the *Pearl*: a number of the characteristics of the child imago appear to derive not from any of its traditional and public manifestations in myth or literature, but directly from the ultimate archetypal sources which manifest themselves solely in private visions and dreams. Such sources can only be tapped in the psychologist's notebooks; though this proceeding may seem somewhat strange and tenuous to the literary scholar, they are too important to the understanding of the pearl maiden to be ignored.

In a study concerning the manifestation of the "child archetype" in the dreams of neurotics and the mental states accompanying such occurrences, C. G. Jung writes:

Visionary experiences of this kind, whether they occur in dreams or in the waking state, are, as we know, conditional on a dissociation having previously taken place between past and present. Such dissociations come about because of various incompatibilities; for instance, a man's present state may have come into conflict with this childhood state, or he may have violently sundered himself from his original character in the interests of some arbitrary *persona* more in keeping with his ambitions. He has thus become unchildlike and artificial, and has lost his roots. All this presents a favourable opportunity for an equally vehement confrontation with the primary truth.

Such may be the causes of the appearance of this figure in the case of neurotic personality. Its manifestation may however be considered a hopeful sign:

But the clearest and most significant manifestation of the child-motif in the therapy of neurosis is in the maturation process of personality induced by the analysis of the unconscious, which I have termed the process of *individuation*.⁹

This process of individuation is associated with particular patterns and types of imagery.

In the individuation process, it [the child figure] anticipates the figure that comes from the synthesis of conscious and unconscious elements in the personality. It is therefore a symbol which unites the opposites; a mediator, bringer of healing, that is, one who makes whole. Because it has this meaning, the child-motif is capable of the numerous transformations mentioned above: it can be expressed by roundness, the circle or sphere, or else by the quaternity as another form of wholeness.¹⁰

Jung writes of the specific transformations:

In dreams [the child] often appears as the dreamer's son or daughter or as a boy, youth, or young girl; occasionally it seems to be of exotic origin, Indian or Chinese, . . . or appearing more cosmically, surrounded by stars or with a starry coronet; . . . Seen as a special

⁹ C. G. Jung and C. Kerényi, *Essays on a Science of Mythology* (New York, 1963), pp. 78, 81.
¹⁰ *Mythology*, p. 83.

instance of "the treasure hard to attain" motif, the child-motif is extremely variable and assumes all manner of shapes, such as the jewel, the pearl, the flower, the chalice . . . It can be interchanged with these and similar images almost without limit.[11]

There are an extraordinary number of resemblances, at once evident, between the poem and the dream experiences reported to Jung. Particularly revealing is the incomplete resemblance between the cause of the dreamer's distress and that of the neurotic. In terms of the "plot" of the poem, the cause of the dreamer's distress must be ascribed to the loss of the pearl, which, as we have shown, has to

[11] *Mythology*, pp. 78–9. Jung's account is not supported by specific evidence of this remarkable association of motifs. His failure to cite the *Pearl* itself among examples of medieval manifestations of the child archetype (*Mythology*, p. 77.) seems proof that he was unacquainted with the work. In *Mythology* itself, there are references to "primordial" children associated with water and flower imagery in C. Kerényi's contributions (pp. 43, 48–9). *Cf.* also Heinrich Zimmer's *Myths and Symbols in Indian Art and Civilization* (New York, 1962), pp. 35–53, especially for the accounts of Narayana, the divine primordial child, a bringer of consolation and enlightenment to the troubled hero. (See also *Mythology*, p. 40.) The alchemical manifestations of the child archetype noted by Jung (*Mythology*, p. 77) may be supplemented by references to Jung, *Psychology and Alchemy* (London 1963), p. 405, *Mysterium Coniunctionis*, (New York 1963), p. 316–21 (on Sir George Ripley's "Cantilena"), and in *The Practice of Psychotherapy* (New York, 1954), pp. 295–9. Manifestations of the archetype in dreams are reported in *The Practice of Psychotherapy*, pp. 44, 183, and in Havelock Ellis, *Studies in the Psychology of Sex* (New York, 1937) II, II, pp. 307–8. This last dream is valuable as originating from a non-Jungian source, as occurring as one of a long series in an exceptionally well documented case, and also as being unusually close to the *Pearl* vision in tone and style; in fact it might be described as a depiction of an abortive attempt to achieve the kind of spiritual transformation embodied in the *Pearl*. Oscar Wilde's story, "The Selfish Giant", comes particularly close to the archetype as described by Jung, though not cited by him. This moving allegory of the *locus amoenus* as the human heart is replete with the symbolism mentioned by Jung: the walled garden contains flowers like stars and blossoms "of pink and pearl", in its first manifestation. Children play there freely. But its giant owner builds a high wall around it, causing perpetual winter to dwell there. One day children creep in through a hole in the wall, and climb the trees, so that the garden is magically transformed into a place of beauty once more. Only in one corner winter still reigns, for the little boy who should climb the tree there is too small to reach it. However, the giant helps the boy into the tree and the frost and snow vanish. One winter, when the giant is very old, he is astonished to see in "the farthest corner of the garden a tree quite covered with lovely white blossoms. Its branches were golden, and silver fruit hung from them, and underneath it stood the little boy he had loved", the one he had helped into the tree. It is the Christ child who has come to take the once selfish

be taken primarily as signifying the death of the dreamer's daughter. Nonetheless, the dreamer's continual failure to understand the nature of the "Kingdom" and his emotional inability to accept the childlike innocence necessary for acceptance there, as opposed to the worthlessness of his hard-earned "merits", permits us to say that "he has become unchildlike and artificial, and has lost his roots."

However, it is hard to see that the dreamer is suffering from some unusual neurosis; surely his imperfect spiritual condition reflects the condition of everyman, while it is the vision prompted by the death of the maiden that reveals to him his spiritual inadequacies. Nevertheless, we may certainly agree that the spiritual distress so occasioned provides, in Jung's words, a favourable opportunity for "a vehement confrontation with the primary truth". Similarly, the appearance of the child figure anticipates and is indeed the primary vehicle for the accomplishment of the "maturation process of the personality" or the spiritual achievements manifested in the poem.

Making full allowance for the differences of approach appropriate to Christian mystic and psychologist, it is clear that they are talking about the same spiritual phenomena. If that is granted, then a peculiar interest attaches itself to the most important differences: for example that it is only through the death of the innocent child that the dreamer attains enlightenment. The *Pearl* seems vastly more complex, subtle and satisfying than anything in psychological theory, even allowing that one is a highly developed work of art and the other a synthesis of neurotic dreams. For in the *Pearl* the archetype and the psychoanalyst are merged into a single figure, whose power to save the dreamer is in some manner dependent on her death. The writings of the psychologist merely describe phenomena associated with the symptoms and the cure of mental distress, whereas the *Pearl* is a work that invites the reader to participate in and actually to undergo the process by which the

---

giant to "my garden, which is Paradise". Wilde's theory of the archetypal in poetry appears in his essay "The Decay of Lying", where he says of Art: "Hers are the 'forms more real than living man', and hers the great archetypes of which things that have existence are but unfinished copies. Nature has, in her eyes, no laws, no uniformity. She can work miracles at her will, and when she calls monsters from the deep they come. She can bid the almond tree blossom in winter, and send snow upon the ripe cornfield."

soul is healed and matured; Jung writes about psychoanalysis, but the *Pearl*, in the deepest sense, is psychoanalysis itself.

Scarcely less illuminating than these correspondences is Jung's observation that the appearance of the child-archetype anticipates the synthesis of conscious and unconscious elements in the personality. Before becoming acquainted with this description of the "individuation" or maturing of the personality, I had been frequently impressed with the way in which medieval allegory depicts, through the combination of rational dialogue and non-rational symbolism, the harmonizing of the claims of reason and the non-rational, or, in more psychological terms, the conscious and subconscious elements. The *Pearl*, as this chapter is intended to show, is one of the works in which such a synthesis can be most clearly demonstrated.

The other points of contact between the *Pearl* and the psychological commentary, referring to specific points of imagery, can be treated more briefly. The roundness of the unifying symbol noted by Jung is paralleled by the insistence of the roundness both of the lost pearl of the opening stanzas "So rounde, so recken in vche araye", and of the pearl of great price "And endeleʒ rounde, and blyþe of mode" (738). We can see the quaternary pattern as a "form of wholenes" in the description of the Heavenly City, which is "abof full sware, As longe as brode as hyʒe ful fayre", as "quaternary" a symbol as anyone could desire. The existence of a father-daughter relationship between dreamer and pearl maiden is first implied in the line, "Ho watʒ me nerre þen aunte or nece" (233), and is confirmed in the previously quoted passages which describe the dwelling of the pearl "in oure þede" and the dreamer's resignation of the pearl to the care of God. An association between the pearl and the orient is made at the opening stanza of the poem ("Oute of oryent, I hardyly saye, Ne proued I neuer her precios pere"). The interchangeability of images that Jung considers especially characteristic of the child-archetype is manifested in the constant transformations of the maiden as pearl, flower (269, 906) and as jewel in respect of her "jeweller" father (stanza group 5). Though there are no stars directly associated with the pearl maiden, the jewels in the river across which she is seen undergo a momentary transformation into stars in the metaphor we have already discussed (115).

The dozen or more correspondences between the two accounts —the poet's and the psychologist's—can hardly be rejected as being without significance, especially as we happen fortunately to have a "control" poem, contemporary to the *Pearl*, Boccaccio's "Olympia" eclogue, in which the poet also has a supernatural vision of his deceased daughter in woodland surroundings. This poem, which is based on the classical eclogue rather than the medieval allegory in form, style and structure, appears to have absolutely no correspondence with the manifestation of the archetype of the child, as described by Jung. Indeed, the poem does not even conclude with the poet receiving any consolation from the vision of his daughter and her description of the beatific life she leads. "In mortem lacrimis ibo, ducamque senectam" (Tearfully towards death I pace, old age leading the way) is his unhappy conclusion. Nor, to look further afield, do there appear to be any correspondences of this type in any classical elegy for a dead child.

What are the implications of this strange series of resemblances between the poet's and the psychotherapist's accounts of the child archetype? We might in the first place reasonably conclude that the *Pearl* poet, as opposed to Boccaccio, based his poem on an actual vision he had experienced or learnt about. These resemblances would seem to constitute additional evidence that medieval allegories are actually sometimes the accounts of personal visionary experiences, as their authors claim.[12] Equally important for our purposes, these psychological characteristics of the child-archetype cast a special light on the symbolic dimensions of literary images. For the interpretation of such images as the pearl the literary historian may trust not only his unaided intuition but also psychological correlatives in assessing the nature and function of their symbolic content.

We can therefore conclude that the pearl maiden in her many transformations is a symbolic manifestation of the dreamer's lost innocence, the innocence that is, in terms of the religious paradox, the key to the kingdom, and, in psychological terms, the reconciliation of the antagonism between the "Resoun" and the "fyrce skylleʒ", the rational and the non-rational elements. The manifestation of the maiden is both a symbol of what the dreamer has lost and an indication that what has been lost may now be found, that the dreamer has been shocked into a state in which he can regain, or at least recognize and come to terms with, what has been lost.

[12] See above, p. 83 and *n*.

Thus the fusion of the "child" figure with that of the more common medieval figure of the "woman in great authority" constitutes a kind of homage to innocence, and at the same time on a more intellectual level a resolution of the paradox that "the first shall be last and the last first", a resolution as convincing imaginatively as intellectually.

But it must nonetheless be insisted that the text allows us little alternative to interpreting the maiden as primarily the poet's daughter; the symbolic roles we have distinguished are no more than aspects of her manifestation which enable us to see her as more than herself, as in a state of glory. Since the interpretations associated with "archetypal" figures always lead one on towards a deeper mystery, and are never completely susceptible to rational explanation, and since the association between figure and meaning is something basic to the realities of the mind rather than merely intellectually constructed, such aspects of the meaning of the pearl maiden seem symbolic rather than allegorical. The figure of the maiden therefore functions (like that of Beatrice) primarily on the literal and symbolic levels, though we may see in each case allegorical meanings such as "comfort, innocence, virginity" loosely associated with her. Beatrice and the pearl maiden represent something of a peak in the development of medieval allegory as a genre. One sees in these figures a perfect balance between realistic concept and nominalistic actuality. All the depth of meaning hitherto reserved for allegorical personifications or Biblical "types" is now available for the enrichment of our understanding of everyday humanity. Unfortunately, the conceptual triumphs represented in the creation of such figures were lost in the iconoclastic excesses of the Reformation.

Conclusion

W HAT value can there be in reading the visionary allegories of the Middle Ages in the present day? Academic purposes apart, this essay has attempted to show that such allegories still have direct potential relevance to contemporary predicaments, especially as we are much less at home in the world of inner experience today than in the Middle Ages. R. D. Laing has written of the problems of the modern schizophrenic:

> The process of entering into the *other* world from this world, and returning to *this* world from the other world, is as natural as death and giving birth or being born. But in our present world, that is both so terrified and so unconscious of the other world, it is not surprising that when "reality", the fabric of this world, bursts, and a person enters the other world, he is completely lost and terrified, and meets only incomprehension in others.[1]

What is needed therefore is:

> Instead of the degradation ceremonial of psychiatric examination, diagnosis and prognostication, . . . an initiation ceremonial, through which the person will be guided with full social encouragement and sanction into inner space and time, by people who have been there and back again.[2]

Or as William Langland expressed the problem in fourteenth-century terms:

> Ac the wey ys wyckede · bot ho so hadde a gyde
> That myght folwen ous ech fot · for drede of mys-tornynge.
> > (*Piers Plowman*, *C*, VIII.307–8)

The kind of help that Laing and Langland call for—the ceremonials, the guides, the charts for voyages into the worlds of inner

---

[1] *The Politics of Experience* (London, 1967), p. 86.
[2] Laing, p. 89.

experience—can be found in medieval allegory. We have seen something of the great range of crises within the inner world covered in such visions. Though the charts seem rather ancient for modern voyages, later ones are hard to find, and their very antiquity is of advantage in assisting us in the essential comprehension of the history of the inner territory. I hope in further writings to show something of the process by which the relatively close medieval association of inner and outer worlds broke down in succeeding centuries; the effects of the resulting psychic dislocation and alienation grow daily more evident around us.

Index

Entries in italic type are literary works used as sources. Numbers in italic type refer to footnotes.

Acheron, 126–30
Aeneid, 25/6, 38, 60, 73, 75; commentary by Bernardus Sylvestris, 76; Aeneas in Elysium, 84, *86*; underworld forests, 113; descent into the underworld, 119–20; transmigration of souls, 135. *See also* Vergil
Aeschylus, 22
agonistes, 33
Alan of Lille: *Complaint of Nature*, 46–68, 85, 89, 93; journey from psychic dislocation to transcendency, 135, 140; *Anticlaudianus*, 84
Alberigo, Friar, *131*
Alcina, 78
Alfonsi, Luigi, 140
allegory: allegory and myth, 1–8; allegory as a genre, 10; allegorical analysis, 15; visionary allegory, 19–21, 41; allegory and symbolism, 42–5; relationship to dialogue, 12, 19, 69; sources of allegorical landscape, 78–83; early Christian allegory, 80; elements of later medieval allegory, 84; allegory in Dante, 116
Allegory of Love, *11*, 33–4, 42–5, 70, *101*, *107*, *142*
Altercatio Ganymedis et Helenae, 97
Altercatio Phyllidis et Florae, 97
ananke, 75
Anchises, 135, 138
Andreas Capellanus, *51*, 79; Palace of Love, 81; *Art of Courtly Love*, 85, 88, 94–8, 105
anguish (psychic crisis): 7, 15; in the *Consolation of Philosophy*, 29; in the *Complaint of Nature*, 47; as prerequisite for visionary allegory, 84; in the *Architrenius*, 87; in twelfth-century allegories, 84; in the *Commedia*, 118; in *Pearl*, 146–8
anti-rational, the, 9, 23
Apocalypse, 151–2
Apuleius, 58, 60
archetype: definition, 14–15; of Lady Nature, 55; of pearl maiden, 156, 160
Architrenius, the, 85–94, 101, 109
Arete, garden of, 80
Ariosto, 78
Aristotle, *17*, *40*, 75
Arthur, King, 105
Attis, 60

Auden, W. H., 6; comment on Dante, *111*
Augustine, St., 36, 79; (Petrarch's), 141–2
Avaritia, 66

Bailey, Cyril, 32
Barfield, Owen, 17, 33
barrier, river: in the *Commedia*, 130; in the *Pearl*, 147–8. *See also* sacred gate
Beatrice, 112, 119, 125, 131–43, 154, 162
Benjamin Minor, 115
Bennett, J. A. W., vii, *53*, *70*
Beowulf, 73–4; garden, 79; enchanted mere, 80
Bernard, St., 133
Bernardus Silvestris (*De Universitate Mundi*), 55, 77, 84; commentary on the *Aeneid*, 13, 76–7, 114
Bernheimer, Richard, 75
Bestiae, 113/14
Blake, William, *45*; *Marriage of Heaven and Hell*, 75
Bland, George, vii
Bloomfield, Morton W., 44
Boccaccio, 161
Bodkin, Maud, 6
Boethius: *Consolation of Philosophy* 21, 28–9; philosophical dialogue, 31–45; Alan's borrowings from, *63*, 66; cosmic contemplation, 84; dictum of Lady Philosophy, 92; 140, 150
Bogdanos, Theodore, vii
Bonaventura, St., 132
Bosch, Hieronymus, 78
Bousset, Wilhelm, *59*
Brady, Ronald, vii
Brooke, Tucker, *142*
Bunyan, John, 89

Camenae, 21, 47
Capellanus, *see* Andreas
Casella, 129
Cassirer, Ernst, 31
Cathars, the, 55–63
Cato, 127–31
Cecil, Evelyn, *100*
Chalcidius, *55*, 75–7
Charon, 126–9
Chartres, school of, 106, 109–10
Chatillon, *see* Gautier

Chaucer, Geoffrey: *Parlement of Foules*, 12, 22, 142; *Book of the Duchess*, *17*; 68, 79; Cave of Morpheus, *House of Fame*, 81, 142; garden in the *Merchant's Tale*, 103–4
Chenu, M. D., *53*
Chrétien de Troyes, 79, 100–101
Christ, 27–8; comfort of Christ, 145; 152–3
Christian imagery, 112–13; early Christian visionary allegory, 80
Cicero, *13*, *17*; dialogues, 32; 138
Circe, 78, 115
city: as landscape symbol, 72; attacked by monster, 73–4; city and wilderness, 99; in the *Pearl*, 150–1
Clare, St., 136
Clementia 12, 24–5
Cligés, 100, 105
Closs, Hannah, 81
cofer, 149
Coleridge, S. T., definition of allegory, 11
Colonna, Francesco, 85
Commedia, 16, *51*; the dark forest, 77; highpoint of medieval allegory, 111; 111–43. *See also* Dante, etc.
Complaint of Nature, 46–68, 85, 93–4, 135–6. *See also* Alan of Lille
Consolation of Philosophy, see Boethius
Cornford, R. M., 54
cosmos and morality, 52, 54
Coulanges, *see* Fustel
Cranach, Lucas, 78
Crisp, Sir Frank, *100*
Cupid, 58, 60, 65, 67–8, 86, 97
Curtius, Ernst R., 37, *40–1*, 56–9, *72*; on ideal landscape, 82
custom (nomos), 54
Cybele, 60
Cyprian, *17*

D'Alverny, Marie, *56*
Damon, Philip W., vii, *17*
Daniel, 5
Dante: attitude to Vergil, 4; Limbo, 92; 111–43; *Dante and Philosophy*, 111; dialogues, 134–8
Dea Syria, 60
Demeter, 58
Democritus, *17*
dialogue: philosophical and classical, 5; between hero and persons in visionary world, 7; role in visionary allegory, 19; classical, 31; therapeutic, 62–7; in the *Complaint of Nature*, 62, 66; landscape and dialogue, 84–110; in Andreas's *Art of Love*, 96; in the *Romance of the Rose*, 107; in the

Divine Comedy, 134–8; dramatic dialogue, 136
Dieu d'Amours, Li Fabel dou, 97, 106
Dirae, 23
discourser, 31; Mistress of Discourse, 21
divisio, *121*
Dodds, E. R., *17*, 71
dogs, hunting, 124
Dominic, St., 132–3
Douglas, Gawain: *Palace of Honour*, 81; *King Hart*, 142
dream interpreters, 5
Dunbar, William, 142

Eden, garden of, 78, 130
eidolon, 12, *17*
Eliade, Mircea, 13, *117*
Elysium: Menelaus's, 82; Vergil's, 84, *86*
enchantress: as peril in the wilderness, 73, 75; enchantresses' gardens, 78
Eumenides, 22
Eliot, T. S., 6
Ellis, Havelock, *158*
erber greene, 144–50
Eunoe, 131
Exodus, 113–14

Faerie Queene, 143, 147
Fama, 26
Fenice, 100, 105
Fletcher, Angus, *4*
Forese, *138*
forest (landscape symbol): 72; perils, 73; in *Beowulf* and *Gilgamesh*, 74; silva and hyle, 75–7. *See also* silva, selva oscura, wilderness
Francesca, 136
Franke, Kuno, *87*
Frye, Northrop, 6
Furies, 22–4
Fustel de Coulanges, 73

garden, 75, 77–8; Garden of Earthly Delights, 78; gardens of Charity and Cupidity, 78–9; literary gardens, 79; secret gardens, 98–105; gardens of love, 98–9; in *Genesis* and the *Song of Songs*, 98; castle gardens, 98–9; hortus conclusus, 98, 101; in Chrétien's *Cligés*, 100; in the *Merchant's Tale*, 103–4; as symbol for private morality, 104–5; in the *Paradiso*, 131–3; erber greene, 144–50; Garden of the Gods in *Gilgamesh*, 147; Bowre of Blisse in the *Faerie Queene*, 147. *See also* park *and* paradise

Gargoyles, 102
Garnerus of St. Victor, 113–15
Gautier de Chatillon, *53, 54*
Gawain, 153
Genesis, 99, 105
Genius (*Romance of the Rose*), 107–8
Gennep, Arnold van, 119–20
Geryon, 125
Gilgamesh, 73–4, 147
Gilson, Etienne, 111–12, 117
Ginguené, Pierre Louis, *87*
Gnosticism, *54*, 59–61, *75*
Golden Bough, the, *75*
Golden Targe, 142
Gordon, E. V., *145*
Gottfried von Strassburg, 104–6
Green, R. H., 46
Grendel, 80, 112
guardians of the river, 125–8
Gudea of Lagash, 1–2, 5
Guillaume de Lorris, 70, 79, 98–105, 136
Gunn, Alan, 107, *109*, 110

Hanville, Jean, *see* John of Hanville
Hastings, *Encyclopaedia of Religion and Ethics*: *54*, 59, *71, 82, 120*
Hell, 80, 119, 121, 124
Henderson, Anne, vii
Henry III, King of England, 100
Hermas: *Pastor of Hermas*, 36, 80, 84, 86, 140, 141
hero, 73–4; in visionary allegory, 84
Hieatt, A. Kent, vii, *145*
Highet, Gilbert, 34
Hinks, Roger, *18, 40*
Hirzel, Rudolf, *36*
Hoffman, Stanton, *154*
Homer, 82
Hous of Fame, 142
Huizinga, Johan, *47*
Huxley, Aldous, 78
hyle, 75–6
Hypnerotomachia, 85

image (imago): mythological imagery, 8; definition of image, 11–14; images used for loci, 13; imago of Lady Philosophy, 36; the Great Mother, 59; development of image in the *Commedia*, 111; symbolic and allegorical imagines, 117; redemption of images, 122–34; pearl maiden, 156
image, seminal: definition, 15; 19–30, 47, 89; in Andreas's *Art of Love*, 94–6, 104; in the *Commedia*, 116; in the *Pearl*, 146–7
incubation, 1, 71
Inferno, 123–5, 128, *131*, 135–7

Ishtar, 54, 57, 59
invocation of the deity, 7, 22, 30
irrational, the, 9
Isaiah, 156
Isis, 60–1

Jackson, W. H., vii
Jacobsen, Th., *2*
Jaeger, Werner, *39*
James, E. O., 57
James I of Scotland, 142
Jean de Meun, 68, 79; Land of Hunger, 81; Abode of Fortune, 81; interpreter of Guillaume de Lorris's garden, 102; *Roman de la Rose*, 105–10
Jeremiah, 113
Jerome, St., 113
Jocus, 60, 64–5, 86
John, St., 132, 145
John of Hanville, Johannes de Altavilla, (Jean de Hautville), 86–94, 136, 140
Johnson, Wendell, *149*
Jonas, Hans, *54*
Joseph, dream interpreter, 5
Jung, C. G.: dream analysis, *3*; description of visionary mode, *5*; 6; archetype of Wise Old Man, 12, 38–9; archetypes, 14–5; child archetype, 157–61
Justin Martyr, 35

Kafka, Franz, 89
Kerényi, C., *157–8*
King Hart, 142
Kingis Quair, 142
Kline, Eric, vii
Knowlton, Edgar, *53*
Koch, Gottfried, *56*
Krouse, F. Michael, *33*

Lage, G. Raynaud de, *53–4*, 66, 70
Laing, R. D., 163
Lamb, the, 153–4
landscape: psychology of, 72ff; landscapes of vision, 69–83; landscape and dialogue, 84–110
Langland, William, 163
Langlois, Ernest, 98
lares, 88–9
Leach, Edmund, *121*
Lethe, river, 131
Lewis, C. S., vii, *11*, 24, 33–4, 42–5, 70; on Guillaume de Lorris, 101; contrast of gardens, 107; imagery of the *Paradiso*, *132*; *142*; The Discarded Image, *148*. See also *Allegory of Love*
Lincoln, J. S., *39*

locus (setting of allegory), 7, 13, 19, 20; relation to abstract ideas, gods, and daimons, 70–1; locus amoenus, 77, 79, 82, 86; locus animae, 78; sources of the imago, 78; types of allegorical loci, 80–3, 91, 105; in the *Architrenius*, 97; Cupid's abode, 97; in the *Commedia*, 135; in Oscar Wilde, *158*

Lorris, *see* Guillaume

love: parodies of, 94–5; *Art of Love*, 94; correct service of, 98; debate on, 98

Lucan, 113

Lucia, 126, 128, 134, 138

Lucian, *82*

Lucretius, *17*

lustrum, *76*

Luttrell, C. A., *144*

Lydgate, John, 83, 142

Lydia, 101

Macdonald, George, *111*

Macrobius, 38

Maggidim, 39

Marlowe, Christopher, 82, 91

masters of discourse, 12

Mater Ecclesia, 141

Matilda, 131, 134

Metamorphoses: (Apuleius), 58, 60; (Ovid), 81–2

metaphor, 21

Methodius, 80–1, 84

Meun, *see* Jean

Mirror of Love, The, 107, *109*

Moira, *54*

Momigliano, Attilio, *118*

monster (beast, daimon): in the *Aeneid*, 26; in the heart, 27; portentum in Prudentius, 27; peril in the wilderness, 73; in *Gilgamesh*, 73; in *Beowulf*, 74, 80; in the *Architrenius*, 87; in the *Comedy*, 111–13; Garnerus's *Bestiae*, 113–14

Montpellier, 56

mother-goddesses, 57, 60

mountain (landscape symbol): Mount of Ambition, 90–2, 112–17; in the *Comedy* and its sources, 124; Mount Purgatory, 140

Muscatine, Charles, vii, 34, *142*

Muses, 21, 29, 40

myth, 1–8

Nanshe, 1, 5

Nature (Natura, Lady Nature): 41–2; *Complaint of Nature*, 46–68, 85–8; as healer, 64; in the *Architrenius*, 91–3; in the *Pearl*, 145; Kynde, *145*

Neckham, Alexander, 91

Nelson, William, vii, 77

Neumann, Erich, 6, *17*

Necessity, 75–6

Ningirsu, 2

nominalism, 143

nomos, 54, *121*

nous, 75, 77, 85, 155

ocean, (landscape symbol), 72

Oedipus, 22–4; *Oedipus Rex*, 113

Oiseuse, 101–2, 151

Olympia, 161

Oppenheim, A. Leo, *2, 4*

Ovid, influence of, 81; *Amores*, 81

Paolo, 136

Papsukkal, 57

paradise, paradise garden, 77–9; of *Genesis*, 99; 101, 140, *159*; Earthly Paradise, 130–1, 134

Paradiso, 131–7

Paris, student life in, 89–91

Park: of Lord Mirth, 70, 78, 98, 151; of the Good Shepherd, 107

Parlement of Foules, 12–22, 70, 142

Parry, J. J., *105*

Pastor of Hermas, see Hermas

Patch, Howard, *81, 91*

Pearl, The, *51*, 136, 142, 144–62

Pearl Maiden, 154–62

pear-tree, *101*, 104

penates, *88*

Persephone (Proserpina), 28, 58

Petroff, Elizabeth, vii

Phaedo, 33

Phaedrus, 84

Pharsalia, 113

Philosophy, Lady, 29, 34–42, 45; dictum of, 92; 140, 150

Piccarda, 135

Piers Plowman, 163

Pietas, 24–5

Plato: inventor of philosophical dialogue, 31; 33; *Laws*, 42; analysis of the universe, 75; concept of necessity, 76

potentia: definition, 12; 13, 16, 19, 20, 26, 30, 32, 37–8, 72; garden as abode of potentia, 80; in Ovid, 81; in twelfth century allegory, 84; in *Romance of the Rose*, 120; 137; Beatrice, 138–41; in *Pearl*, 156

potestas, *13*

pre-rational, the, 7–9

Pritchard, James B., 58

Proserpina, *see* Persephone

Prudentius: *Psychomachia*, 27–8; 63, 65; *Contra Orat. Symmachi*, 28; *Harmartigenia*, 86; 112, 123, 142
Psyche, 58, 60
psychoanalysis, 3, 5, 6
psychological postulates, 16–18
Psychomachia, 7, 9, 27–8, 112, 123, 142
Purgatorio, 124, 128–9, 131, 135, 137, 138

questioner, 31
Quintilian, 21

Raj, Myrtle, vii
Reason (Resoun, Lady Reason): 117, 139, 140; in the *Pearl*, 145; 150, 155, 161
Richard of St. Victor, 17, 115
Robertson, D. W., 79, 101
Robinson, F. N., 142
Romance of the Rose (*Romaunt of the Rose, Roman de la Rose*): 44, 70, 78, 86; Daunger, 98; 101–10; 139, 149, 151–2
Rosa, Lady, 141
Rougemont, Denis de, 57
Runciman, Steven, 56

sacred gate: in the *Divine Comedy*, 120, 130–1. *See also* barrier
sacred places, 70–2
Sanctis, Francesco De, 111
Sayers, Dorothy L., 126
Sapegno, 126
Scaglione, Aldo, 56
Schless, Howard, vii
Scipio, 12, 138
Scotus Erigena, 53
selva oscura: in the *Divine Comedy*, 112–13, 122–5, 129, 130; selva selvaggia, 111–17, 124. *See also* silva *and* forest
seminal image, *see* image
Seneca, 113
Servius, 75–7
sex, 67–8; sexual perversity, 51, 56, 59–64, 67
Shumaker, Wayne, 9
Sibyl, 119
Siena, 131
silva, 75–7, 85. *See also* selva *and* forest
Singleton, Charles, 122, 126
Snell, Bruno, 33
Socrates, 12; teaching methods, 31; last hours, 33; conversation with Phaedrus, 84
Solon, 92
Somnium Scipionis, 12, 138; *Somnium* (of Lucian), 82

Song of Songs, 78, 99, 101, 105
Sophia, 59, 61
Sordello, 137
Spenser, Edmund, 22, 30; Spenser's allegorical figures, 143. *See also* the *Faerie Queene*
Statius, 22, 25–6, 88, 91
Streitgedicht, 97
Strassburg, *see* Gottfried
Styx, river, 89
Sumerian: dream, 2; *ensi*, 4; incubation, 1, 71; Dilmun paradise, 82
Sun, 112
symbol: in the *Divine Comedy*, 171
symbolism: definition, 8–9; 11, 19, 20; allegory and symbolism, 44–5; child in the *Pearl*, 156
Symposium of Methodius, 80–1, 84

Tamburlaine, 91
Telepinus, 58
Tempe, vale of, 72
Temple of Glas, 142
terms, definition of, 8–18
Thebaid, 22, 24, 88, 91
Theodorus, 72
The Thrissil and the Rois, 142
Thule, 90, 91–2
Theodotus, the Montanist, 72
Tillyard, E. M. W., 114
Timaeus, 75–6
Tisiphone, 23, 25, 44
tradition in allegory, 16
Tristan, 105
Troilus, 137
Trumbull, H. C., 120
Tuve, Rosemond, 26, 109, 143

Usener, H., 39, 71

Vallone, Aldo, 126
Venus: 44, 60–1, 64; Venus scelesta, 66–8; girdle of, 92; in the *Romance of the Rose*, 107–8
Vergil: Dante's attitude to, 4; Fama, 25–6; significance of silva, 76; underworld, 86; in the *Commedia*, 112; Vergilian categories, 117–22; Vergil as Dante's rescuer, 117, 125–7, 137
Veritas, Lady, 141–2
vices, 65
virtues, 65
Virgin Mother, 59, 61
Vita Nuova, 139

Walther, Hans, 97
Wellek, Rene, 154

Werblowsky, R. J., *39*
Wetherbee, Winthrop, vii
Wheelwright, Philip, *22*
Wicksteed, P. H., *126*
Wilde, Oscar, *158*
wilderness and city, *72–8*, 99
Williams, Gwyn, *72*
Winden, J. C. M. van, *75*
Wright, Thomas, *47*, 86

wyrd, 149, 150

Xenocrates, 92
Xenophon, *82*, *86*

Yeats, W. B., 6

Zimmer, Heinrich, 158
Zion, 114